Reiki & Other Rays of Touch

Presented by the Healing Arts Series
Kathleen Ann Milner

Reiki & Other Rays of Touch Healing

by Kathleen Milner

Chapter Outline

Tera-Mai
™

Release

Acknowledgements

Introduction

Tera-Mai
TM

It is my personal belief that we are given freewill choice so that we can learn our lessons within a certain framework which we describe here on planet Earth as the third dimension. In our learning process Mother-Father God is like the good school teacher or good government; that is, one who has only a few rules, but those rules are purposeful and designed with the intention that they are for the common good of all. We refer to God's rules as sacred law. I believe that the Reiki initiations retrieved by Dr. Usui fit into the definition of sacred law. Madam Takata was probably well intentioned *(aren't we all?)* when she decided to charge $10,000 for the Reiki Mastership initiation and alter the Reiki initiations. I know this to be true because I have reinitiated and spoken with Reiki Masters who are one step away from the source. For whatever their reasons, they share the Reiki initiations that they have received and are teaching. I personally believe that Madam Takata's decision laid the foundation for the confusion in Reiki today. I also believe that, for whatever the reason, this did have a higher purpose.

It is my personal belief that the highly evolved being who appeared to Marcy Miller and myself initially as brown skinned, dressed in orange, and wearing an Afro hairstyle had found the same Universal empowerment, Universal symbols and Universal knowledge that Dr. Usui had when he made his conscious raising journey into the inner planes. I also believe that the Reiki lineage (showing Dr. Usui's name and the names of the other Reiki Masters who came before) that is given to Reiki Masters at the time of their initiation, is actually a legal contract. The initiations I give and teach have been expanded upon by what I believe to be higher spiritual forces. Thus, if my name appeared on a Reiki lineage, one would believe that the empowerment and knowledge of the three Reiki initiations that they were being given was the same as those that I describe in my videos, lectures and this book, <u>Reiki & Other Rays of Touch Healing</u>.

To aid individuals in their search for either another Reiki system or the one I describe herein, I have trademarked the name **Tera-Mai™**. **Tera-Mai™** *Reiki* and **Tera-Mai™** *Seichem* can be used by teachers in their advertising, certificates, etc. only when they have been initiated into, and are initiating individuals (one on one - teacher focuses attention on and initiates one person at a time), and teaching the initiations in a specific manner as described on the <u>Reiki Mastership</u> video. **Tera-Mai** ™ is the name which my angels and spirit guides call this golden elemental earth ray of healing energy. I believe that all elemental healing rays come from Source or Mother-Father God, and to give healing energy any human being's name is actually limiting. Healing rays are Universal; for as a sign that this is truth, Spirit reveals this knowledge to me in visions of old texts which are bound in crow feathers.

Release

Kathleen Milner is not a medical specialist capable of diagnosing or prescribing. She works with symptoms and healing energies, and she is a channel of healing energy which facilitates self-healing and she can neither be responsible for, nor can she guarantee the form the healing may or may not take. <u>Reiki & Other Rays of Healing</u> is not a substitute for conventional medical treatment.

Acknowledgements

My book is about healing and elemental healing rays of energy which emanate from Mother-Father God. Within these pages can be found many healing techniques, including some basic instruction given in Reiki I and II classes. It is also about my journey back to health and Wholeness, and my work on the inner planes with Sai Baba, other masters and angels.

My particular road to perfect health has been slower than most of the people whom I have helped. In looking back I can see that my healing unfolded in such a manner that I might be guided to learn as much as possible from many different teachers, exponents of different schools of thought. In God's wisdom I learned to become a channel of His/Her healing and not to be full of myself.

The goal of this book is to make the invisible real, to demystify abstract constructs of how the manifestation of healing transformations takes place, tie-in related aspects from different spiritualisms, and offer glimpses into other possibilities. Towards the achievement of these objectives I owe a debt of gratitude to all of my teachers, and to my students, who have also served as my teachers. For the greater part I have been truly blessed by the quality of students who have come to me. Many of my students have gone on to be established healers, teachers, authors and speakers in their own right. I thank Jeremiah Brod and his guides for contributing to the chapter on color. I thank Straight Arrow, who came to me when I was 7-years-old and saved my life, and who has been my guardian ever since. I thank my dear friend, Abez, who came to me in my time of great need, and who carried me on his strong back through many of my life's difficulties. I thank Sai Baba for the knowledge he shared from the inner planes. I thank my dear friend, Marcy Miller, who first brought Sai Baba's wisdom to me. I thank my friend, Jackie, who helped me edit this book. I thank my friend, Charlotte Liss, who carefully proof-read. I thank my children, Lee and Jennifer Owrey, for their unconditional love and support. I thank my parents, Marian and Joseph, for the gifts I was born with. I am grateful for the many generous souls who have helped me in very practical ways on my journey.

In addition I would like to thank all of the wonderful people who purchased the first edition; thus, making this second edition possible. There were a few errors that were missed in the final rush to get the first edition printed that have been corrected, and I have further clarified a few ideas, and added additional examples and healing techniques. As this edition contains the same number of pages as the first, the major difference between the two is that, like completing a marble statue, the arms and the rest of the structure are not altered but the rough edges are worked out and polished. As the pages are now full, I find myself looking at a second book, Tera, My Journey Home. I knew what cover I was to use for Reiki & Other Rays of Touch Healing before I started writing the book. I now know the painting I am to use for Tera, My Journey Home. It is time to begin writing.

The constructive criticism I received from the first edition was that the chapter on animals focused too much on horses. If you can find a good comparative anatomy book, what I say about horses is applicable to other species as well. The third companion video to this book, Healing Animals, has more of a variety of 4-legged, but the emphasis is still on horses.

Some people commented that I didn't smile in the first two companion videos, Healing Hands and Symbols in Healing. I was intently focused on getting as much information as I could to those who purchased the videos. My respect and understanding goes out to those who make their living by standing in front of a camera, which has the same demanding exactitude as an army sergeant. I did ask the director to remind me to smile when we filmed Healing Animals. This video contains a great deal of information as well as being artistically pleasing.

Thank you Mother-Father God for Your Blessings, Your Mercy and the wonder You have shown me.

Introduction

Healing affirms the reality of other dimensions and of the presence of God Him/Herself. In some diabolical twist, healing and the other psychic gifts Jesus performed and taught to his disciples and furthermore instructed them to teach to others, have become looked upon in some quarters as the work of the devil. Nowhere in any version of any bible, in either the Old or New Testament is the devil given credit for healing anyone. Jesus said, "Ye shall do greater things than I have done." One of the Gifts of the Spirit is healing others (Luke 9 Verse 2, Luke 10 Verse 9, Matthew 10 Verse 8). Jesus lived and died 2,000 years ago, and perhaps it is now time for us to at least examine the possibilities.

Mother-Father God loves each one of us unconditionally. It is our responsibility, however, to make the effort to find the way back home. To find 'heaven' we use our gifts to seek the knowledge and love of the Oneness. Knowledge that we are a part of the One brings about Wholeness. We are here to find the Truth of our own individual beingness and of our relationship with All There Is. There is more to both us and God's creation than we dare to believe. Albert Einstein proved that everything is energy. We are energy; we are multidimensional beings. Our consciousness resides in other realities besides here on earth.

Not seeking the knowledge is what shackles us and makes us slaves. We need to be able to focus and pay attention on our 'earth walk,' yet at the same time we should be able to shift into these other realities, much the same as newborns and the very elderly do, only with intention and purpose. When we loose sight of these other dimensions we severely limit our possibilities. Trinity is like a triangle: Oneness, Wholeness and Truth are at each of the points, and within the center is Mother-Father God.

Buddha instructed his followers not to 'buy into' everything he told them. He said, question! Meditate on the possibilities! Live it and see what works for you! Ask God for confirmation of the Truth so that you might know it for yourself! This is what I invite you to do with my book, for I realize that there will be passages and concepts that will be a stretch to your consciousness. When you find things herein that do work for you, and it feels right to do so, use them in your own healing process.

History of Reiki

One hundred years ago Mikao Usui sought knowledge of enlightenment. Most of what we know about Usui comes from a few western books. Books on Usui usually tell of how he was a Christian, who turned to Eastern teachings when he was unable to find out how Jesus performed his healings and miracles in Christian doctrines and texts. That at one point he had even gone so far as to earn a doctorate of theology at the University of Chicago, which is why he is commonly called Dr. Usui There is a problem. The University of Chicago has neither records of his graduation, nor of his even attending the school.

I have gleaned insights from countless individuals. This has compelled me not only inwards to question and ask for the Truth, but also to study with teachers, healers and shamans in a variety of workshops, seminars and classes. The classrooms have been held in a wide range of locations from posh hotels in New York City, to the jungles of the Yucatan. From my journey of self healing and discovery, what follows herein is what I personally feel to be true about Reiki, healing and Mikao Usui:

Mikao Usui's journey was lifelong. Unable to find knowledge of healing in translations of the Sutras, Master Buddha's teachings, he sought out the original version. Here was to be found the wisdom of healing and means of empowerment. Earth has been held bound with dark, heavy energy, so Universal concepts were not spelled out in detail anywhere for anyone to see, learn and misuse. Ancient doctrines and truths masked in rich Sanskrit verse waited for the right time and the pure of heart to decipher spiritual codes.

Mikao Usui was a Buddhist monk. However, Buddha's Sutras were not available for loan to another country, no matter how aspiring the student or how noble the quest! Thus, Usui's search led him to India, Mongolia and Tibet to master Sanskrit and study with the Tibetan monks. Afterwards he spent considerable time reading these venerable manuscripts. Sacred law was revealed to him in much the same way as when we read the Bible, suddenly finding ourselves in an expanded state of mind when we are presented with and know the Truth. Universal mysteries reached out beyond the passages to Usui's inner knowing and to his remembering. In another lifetime he had been one of the Tibetan masters.

Mikao Usui had found his answers. However, wisdom without the power to implement it, is like trying to catch water with a sieve. You know you have something, but you can never get a hold of it. In order to be able to manifest the full knowledge of healing, transformation and manifestation, he had to go through a conscious raising experience.

A conscious raising experience entails considerably more than most people would imagine. In order to grasp this concept, let us look to Egypt. Whenever a pyramid is opened and archaeologists go into the Pharaoh's ornate burial chamber, they always find two things. That is, the pharaoh is buried in another part of the pyramid; the other is the discovery of air holes in the sarcophagus. Air holes are the last thing a society intent on preserving its dead would drill into coffins. The reason behind these two mysteries is quite simple. The King's Chamber in the pyramid is not a tomb; the empty coffin is actually an initiation chamber. An initiation chamber with multiple covers or lids, allowing precious little air in and absolutely no circulation. A chamber where the aspiring initiate would lie in a high state of sustained meditation for three days; a state of meditation so deep that very little oxygen was required to sustain life. It was in this condition that the successful initiate was rewarded with the ultimate prize; s/he retrieved not only psychic knowledge, but the power to perform advanced metaphysical tasks and healing abilities.

What are referred to as Mayan funerary pyramids are oftentimes initiation chambers. While the King's chamber in Egypt's great pyramid at Cheops is 2/3's of the way up, the initiation room at Palenque is below the ground level of the pyramid (pyramids have a mirror image constructed directly underneath of them). At Palenque the chamber (after the priests helped the initiate achieve a deep trance state) was covered with a large, inscribed stone, which is still there for visitors to see. As in Egypt, once the process had begun there was no turning back.

Maintaining a high state of meditation in a confined chamber for 72 hours is not an initiation one embarks upon lightly or haphazardly. There was no possibility of escape; the lids were raised only after the allotted time period. Prospective initiates would prepare themselves for years; through study, by practicing meditation and going through many minor initiations. One of these minor initiations was swimming the crocodile-infested Nile River to reach an underwater entrance to a temple on the opposite bank. The initiate had to put all fear aside, for that emotion would only sound out as clearly as a dinner bell at the initiate's expense. I have one student who has past life recall of going through this initiation, making it to the other side, only to find that a fellow student in his jealousy refused to open the door. Too exhausted to swim back, the once hopeful initiate drown.

Even if the aspiring initiate had the emotional, mental and physical skills to make it through the minor initiations, there was no guarantee of surviving the initiation in the King's Chamber. Another of my students came to the realization in a past life regression that she had unsuccessfully attempted the initiation in the King's Chamber. At the time she knew instinctively that she was not yet ready. However, rather than listening to her own inner knowing, she went ahead anyway and died as a consequence. One of her lessons in this lifetime has been to learn to listen to her intuition.

In Egypt the royal family and elite, as well as the religious, state and secular leaders had access to the metaphysical schools of initiation and instruction. It was not only considered an honor to be able to go through these schools, but it was expected of the Pharaoh and those in line of succession. Egyptians always used their left brain library knowledge as well as their right brain intuition in all highly involved tasks, be it engineering, embalming or leadership. How could the the physician perform surgery or the pharaoh rule without having developed all higher mental skills?

Moses as a baby had been found by the Pharaoh's oldest daughter, who was without child, and she raised Moses as her own. The Pharaoh's oldest son always married the Pharaohs oldest daughter. This singular fact places Moses as first in line to the throne of Egypt, which means that Moses would have had to have gone through all of the initiations and learned all of the metaphysical teachings available in Egypt. After Moses led the Hebrews out of Egypt his name was erased from all of the stones, monuments and documents, so we do not know for certain whether or not he was actually Pharaoh. In the bible we also find testimony to the fact that Moses was an accomplished metaphysician. The story of Moses and the Amman high priests transforming sticks into snakes is not a story of mass hypnosis, but rather a tale of dueling alchemists. Moses and the priests were literally altering the vibration and changing the mass from stick to snake. The jurisdiction of all alchemists is their mastery over all four elements - earth, air, fire and water. When Moses parted the Red Sea, as an alchemist he was demonstrating his command over one of the four elements, water, and used the combined force of elemental power to manifest his intent.

Moses taught the Hebrews, who had been "chosen" to learn sacred mysticism and to keep the ancient lore of Mother-Father God, the secrets of Egypt. It was after Moses taught the Jews that they transformed from a simple nomadic culture to a viable force in the Middle East. Moses then climbed a mountain and returned with white hair. The reason for the change in hair color is because Moses had been gone for a long time. Moses had actually journeyed to India, Mongolia and Tibet in order to extend his mystical learning and understanding. Upon returning as an elderly man with added knowledge of sacred laws, he discovered that many of the Hebrews were abusing the Universal energy in their own way, just as the Egyptians and Atlantians had done previously. It is our birthright to be co-creators of the Universe; however, we are expected to work out of love and joy, and respect for all of the rest of creation. When we don't, our gifts are taken away. We are sent back to learn the basics. Once again in human history the "Law had been defiled." It was then that the mystical secrets were handed down orally through a Jewish sect called the Essenes. It is no coincidence that Mary, Joseph, Jesus, John the Baptist and Lazarus were all Essenes. Jesus was called the Nazarean because that was the sect within the Essenes that he belonged to.

Lazarus was the last man on earth to go through the three-day initiation of sustained high meditation I described earlier. Lazarus' sisters had sent for Jesus so that he might bring their brother back from "the land of the dead." Yet, when Jesus arrived, he was told that he was too late, "Lazarus is dead." Lazarus had been unable to break the state of suspended animation by himself and his physical body perished. Jesus then performed his second greatest miracle, raising Lazarus' dead body. Later, Jesus would perform the ultimate miracle; laying down his own body and resurrecting it back to life.

Looking again at the bible, we are told that at Jesus' birth the Magi, who were wealthy magicians, astronomers and astrologers, had been following a star. Utilizing the historical clues from the Bible itself, the University of Wisconsin's astronomy department speculates in a program, they put on at Christmastime, that Jesus was born 13 years earlier than 1 AD (which also means that we have been in the year 2,000) and that the Magi were following the king planet Jupiter. Upon entering Bethlehem the constellation of the Virgin hung over the city. These three magi then gave Mary and Joseph, a skilled carpenter, expensive gifts of gold, frankincense and myrrh. Jesus is the Greek translation for the Hebrew name, Joshua (God is salvation). He was born in a humble stable in Bethlehem so that the prophesies might be fulfilled, "and David will walk among you in the city of Bethlehem." Which could be taken that Jesus is a reincarnation of King David.

Jesus and his family were not poor. In his day, Saint Francis' poverty was a discomfort to the pope, cardinals and clergy, who were living high on the hog by selling indulgences and church offices. Some papacies had a monopoly running and operating all of the whore houses in Rome. Church officials thought that Saint Francis was embarrassing them. In stark contrast to Saint Francis' goodness and poverty, they felt he called attention to their promiscuity and opulent lifestyles. It was after Saint Francis' death that poverty would be promoted by the church. They discovered that asking the masses to emulate Jesus' supposed poverty made it easier to secure donations from the faithful.

To protect their son from Herod, Jesus' parents used their wealth to flee into Egypt and educate their son. In Egypt Jesus received instruction in the Egyptian temples. As a young man he studied in India, Mongolia and Tibet. India's legend of Saint Isa is the story of Jesus, who was called back to Jerusalem at the age of 33 when his father died.

Jesus' true teachings were altered by ignorant Romans beginning in the third century after Constantine conquered Rome and incorporated the church into the state. In 553 A.D. the Roman church-state began taking out all references to reincarnation in the New Testaments; however, there are some they missed. For example, Jesus talked about one of the caesars being caesar twice (there was never an overthrow of a caesar and a subsequent climb back to power). Jesus' disciples asked him if he was Elija, and rather than reprimanding them for believing in reincarnation, he responded by saying that John the Baptist had been Elija. Reincarnation was vehemently rejected by the Church-state because they found out that they could not control a population who did believe in it. They wanted to insure that the masses would look to and pay the Church for their salvation. (Reincarnation: The Phoenix Fire Mystery compiled and edited by Joseph Head and S. L. Cranston) Balloting, by one vote they made Jesus divine. It was a stroke of genius! By making Jesus more than he ever claimed to be; that is, the only son of God, he was placed upon a pedestal for our admiration, never our emulation. The Messiah means the chosen one. The one who would lead the people out of darkness and into the knowledge of Oneness.

Ways and means of developing psychically are found within Jesus' original teachings. The original manuscripts (there are over 50) are currently locked away in a chapel in the Vatican. Jesus' teachings were still available in the 3rd century when Saint Patrick brought the knowledge and ability to heal to Ireland. Men and women referred to as saints by the church have demonstrated psychic skills. Most of them, a discomfort to the Church while living, were uplifted to unearthly status after their deaths. Again the masses would never think that they, too, could possibly strive for nonordinary accomplishments and abilities. One would have to be an egomaniac to think such thoughts.

The Holy Inquisition, ordered by the pope, was an attempt by the Roman Catholic Church to silence women who, like Joan of Arc, worked with spirit, herbs and the feminine aspect of God. The other victims were the Essenes, those who carried on the mysticism that had been given to them by Moses and later added onto by Jesus. During this period 9,000,000 European women met their deaths. It was a woman's holocaust around which a whole economic structure was based. It took only one accusation by one individual to set off a whole chain of events. People were paid to find and get the witch, to hold her in captivity, to torture her, lawyers and judges had to be paid, and those who murdered her were also paid. The defendant had no defence. Their accuser was never revealed, and they were not even informed of what it was that they were even accused of. The guilty were either burned alive at the stake, tortured to death, or drowned. To pay for all this and to add to the coffers of those in power, the witch's property and that of her relatives was seized. To escape the Holy Inquisition and to protect their families, to this day in Europe there are stories of the gathering of hundreds upon hundreds of women. "Holding hands, in a refusal of betrayal, chanting to the Mother Goddess chose their deaths in the sea." (Christy Moore, Burning Times) "In this age of evil," while it was not unheard of to burn children and even whole towns, the majority of the remaining 2 million people burned were men, Essene mystics.

Under heavy Catholic control, the burning laws were not even taken off the books in Ireland until the 1940's. Witch trials began in Massachusetts, but with the need for women in the wilderness, and with other colonies like Virginia outlawing the practice, the witch trials halted. The United States Bill of Rights insured individual freedom and the right to a fair trial in the new world. The separation of church and state guaranteed that the Roman Catholic Church would not control American politics the way it had in Europe. Popes literally dethroned or controlled monarchs. The Three Musketeers and In the Name of the Rose only scratch the surface of Church political and social interference (Peter De Rosa, The Vicars of Christ, The Dark Side of the Papacy). The founding fathers never intended to take God out of the state.

The point is that one-hundred years ago the only ancient documents on healing and spiritualism left unaltered and available were Buddha's Sutras. After studying the same passages Jesus had read 1,900 years earlier, Usui realized that he, too, had to attain a high altered state of consciousness in order to be empowered with healing energy. He was then guided to return to Japan where he climbed to the top of one of the mountains. The mountains in Japan are sacred. There he meditated and fasted for 21 days, at the end of which time, he was literally struck in his third eye by a bolt of lightning. In his own unconsciousness he became conscious to the healing rays from Mother-Father God that he had searched for.

Upon awakening he discovered healing vibrations strongly emanating from his hands. He also knew how, and was capable of transferring elemental healing energies of earth, air, fire and water through a series of initiations. These were the same initiations that Jesus gave to his disciples. It was in this manner that Jesus transformed illiterate fishermen (the only educated apostles were Mark, a tax collector and Luke, a physician) into master healers and knowledgeable metaphysicians in a relatively brief period of time. Trials and tribulations their ancestors endured in ancient Egypt to attain enlightenment were no longer necessary. Jesus, the shower of ways, provided a means for anyone to achieve God Consciousness; a way ultimately to end the reincarnation cycle and death itself.

Mikao Usui then began his healing mission and he initiated other men into the elemental healing rays. They were called Reiki (energy) Masters because they, like the alchemists before them, had command over all of the Universal elemental forces of earth, air, fire and water of which we ourselves are composed. It is the nature of the hologram that all parts are in relationship to all other parts. The forces that combine and bind the energy of the four elements provides a theme in variation in our holographic universe. One simple example of this phenomenon is that earth and air both have the ability to hold water but in different forms. Elements are multidimensional in that they exist on this planet, other planets and other planes of existence; and within each one of the elements is a ray of healing. Japanese Reiki Masters, masters of the Chi, were capable of performing miracles because they could work on all aspects of the human body and subtle bodies. Misqualified energy had no where to run so to speak.

Stories of the healing miracles of the Reiki Masters reached the ears of Hawayo Takata, a Japanese American woman living in Hawaii. She was dying of cancer. Taking the risk, she went to Japan and was healed her of her disease. She expressed her gratitude, and then relentlessly begged them to initiate and teach her Reiki. Dr. Chujiro Hayashi at last obliged. It was the 1930's and Takata was not a man, do you really think they told her everything? Perhaps not even today would a woman be told everything. In addition there is an old Oriental tradition, that of the master withholding from his students. After initiating her, the Japanese masters gave Takata the symbols and initiation procedures for the healing ray from element earth only, because without the grounding of earth, nothing else is going to happen. For whatever her reasons, Takata thought they had given it all to her.

Takata returned to Hawaii. When she was able to, she began practicing the ancient art of laying on of hands, or facilitating healing. She was both proficient and popular, and like the Japanese men, she charged for her services. When people ask me, "Why should I have to pay for healing that comes from God?" I answer that everything comes from Mother-Father God; musical talents are also a gift, yet Van Clyborn does not leave the concert hall unpaid. Most concert pianists and healers spend time developing their legacy. There needs to be some kind of energy exchange on the part of the healee; something for nothing does not exist. If something is offered free on a silver platter, look again, it's probably tin. On the other hand, and equally important, healing work or anything that is done foremost for monetary reasons is destined to failure. As Sai Baba says, "Work for the love of God and leave the fruits of your labor to Him." Or as Julia Cameron, author of the Artist's Way, says, "artists supply the quantity, God supplies the quality."

People then began begging Takata for the information and abilities to heal and teach others. She did not think that Americans were ready for all of the power that she had received from Dr. Hayashi. She was probably right! Albert Einstein had the same doubts concerning his work after seeing what the individuals behind the world powers did with Nicola Tesla's work in the Philadelphia Experiment; and their corresponding failure to develop the free electromagnetic energy found within earth herself. I have heard from several sources that Einstein decided not to release all of his theories or all of the proofs to his theories.   Takata solved her problem by simply leaving out over half of the initiation procedure and a symbol for each of the three Reiki degrees. To go one step further she priced the third degree, Reiki Mastership, at ten-thousand American dollars, a sum of money at that time, and even in this day, large enough to discourage many aspiring students. Her intent was to protect Reiki and at the same time make it available.

Takata initiated twenty-two Reiki Masters in her lifetime. The proof of my words lies in the fact that not even one of these masters, including her own granddaughter, are capable of facilitating the same kinds of miracles that Mikao Usui or even Takata were able to perform. Every now and again there have been sudden and dramatic healings, but not on any kind of a regular and consistent basis. All of the Reiki Masters know this, all of them know that something was left out. Later after I began to reinitiate Reiki Masters from each of these 22 lineages, I discovered that in some cases there were subtle differences in what Takata had taught each of them. She was only following in the tradition of her teachers, giving more to one student than to another.

In order to retrieve the complete wisdom and empowerment of all of the elemental rays, we cannot return to Japan and learn from the Reiki Masters that Mikao Usui initiated. As a point of honor, those who had been fully initiated committed suicide by the blade just prior to World War II so that the Japanese empire could not misuse the energy for world conquest. Unknown to them, Mikao Usui, was guided to protect the sacred knowledge by not telling his students everything he knew. It was his destiny to initiate a process, not to complete it.

The Reluctant Reiki Master

I was unaware of the Reiki drama when I became initiated eleven years ago. In 1983, after watching a Reiki demonstration, I was initiated into the first two Reiki degrees. Originally I thought I had become involved for three reasons. There had always been energy in my paintings and drawings from the time I was a little girl. I was impressed to see if the initiations would add healing qualities to my art work. Secondly, devotion is a part of my nature and I wanted to be closer to Mother-Father God. What better way to express my nature than to again channel healing energies? Thirdly, it gave meaning to extraordinary experiences I had had as a young girl and woman. When I was young the fact that I could pray for someone and virtually see a change overnight scared me. I never prayed for myself because at a very young age I had been told by a nun that that was selfish. When I prayed as a little girl, I also asked that God's Will be done because another nun had impressed that upon me. One of the most important things Reiki gave to me was the full understanding that I was not responsible for another person's healing or lack thereof. Reiki healing involves God, Holy Spirit and the individual in question. I was only the facilitator!

In reading books on healing in the 18th and early 19th century, the healer had to be aware not to contract the disease s/he was healing his/her client of. There was also the danger of the healer giving of their own energy. In the movie, Resurrection, based on the life of a healer, Ellen Burstein, the healer, gets into the hospital bed of a woman with spasmodic seizures. While a host of medical professionals watch, the woman slowly stops and Ellen slowly starts moving uncontrollably. It took a week for the healer to recover. As Reiki healing energy comes from Universal Source, I am neither drained of my own energy nor do I contract the diseases of others.

After the first two Reiki initiations, I would have liked to have gone on and completed the third initiation, but not wishing to ransom my two wonderful children, I put aside the idea of becoming a Reiki Master, I thought, forever. Forever proved a short time in coming, for in 1988 after two automobile accidents, I was left at a standstill with my artwork and my life. I had just found a gallery in Chicago to represent me; but I was left frustrated and closed down with a concussion and brain trauma. I also suffered from severe muscle spasms. While my doctor was advanced and went so far as to prescribe massage therapy, stretch exercises and rolfing, I was still in severe pain. Sometimes it would literally take me an hour to get out of bed in the morning.

Then in the summer of 1989 I received a brochure from a new age retreat, the Haven, in Walkerville, Michigan. Reiki Mastership was one of the workshops offered; not for $10,000 but for the reasonable cost for a weekend class. I did not question how this could be possible, I simply knew it was right. For my own healing process, I had to go. I told several friends, who were Reiki practitioners, about it but because the class was offered over Thanksgiving weekend none of them could get away. So I made holiday arrangements for my two children with their father and my exhusband, and went alone. Once there I made some friends, had a good time and walked in the woods of this once girl scout camp. It was one of those beautiful places in nature willed and entrusted to an organization that supposedly would preserve the wilderness forever and later sold. I was initiated into the third level of Reiki, learned how to do the initiations, and began a cleansing cycle for my own healing. Mistakenly, I thought that was the end of it, and I kept my little secret to myself.

One day during that winter the thought occurred to me that I had paid a lot of money and traveled a long ways to take Reiki Mastership. The initiation had released and healed much of my pain. I pondered on the possibility of utilizing it further in my life. The breathing technique which is used to do the initiations had been taught, but not stressed. I was to discover later that Takata herself never emphasized the breathing in her teachings, and while she taught it to most of the Reiki Masters, she did not teach it to everyone. In thinking back to the class, I recalled how difficult and how much energy it took for me to do the breathing. Anything that is worthwhile doing takes practice, so I started doing it a few times a day. I was not even sure why. I was literally impelled from within.

That March a young man held a crystal workshop in my home. One of his students, Michelle Lichtman, was an acquaintance whom I had seen at other metaphysical functions and classes. My daughter, Jennifer, was also in the class. And sometime during the course while we worked in front of the fireplace, Jennifer told Michelle, "My mother's a Reiki Master." With those words, my own daughter changed the whole course of my life. To this day I can see Michelle's face. Her mouth was open so wide that you could count all of her teeth. When she discovered that I did not pay $10,000, and that I could initiate her and teach her how to do the initiations, she asked me what it would take for me to teach her. I thought for a moment and told her that if she could get 3 other people together, that I would put together a class.

I have two college degrees, one is in elementary education and I have taught both the first grade and higher level reading skills in college. I had several goals in mind for the class. Since experimenting with the breathing, I was convinced that it was important and should be

10

highlighted. While I learned what I needed to in Michigan, my personal teaching preference was to incorporate more structure into the class than I had experienced. At the same time I wanted to make the class fun and enjoyable. Later I discovered a way in which to use the ancient symbols from Egypt and those of the Rune Masters to teach the breathing.

My first Reiki Mastership class was set in April of 1990, and rather than 4 students, I ended up with 6. I would have had 7, but one woman had already made arrangements to fly to Texas that weekend. To accommodate her, I set up another class on a weekend the following month and ended up with 8 students in that class. Another 4 women made their own arrangements with me to teach them the following Monday and Tuesday. And so it went through the summer with people calling me and asking me to teach them, until my very own Judas came unsuspectingly into my life and into my classroom.

By the summer of 1990 I was teaching Reiki I, II and III and Judas took all three classes. During sharing times after the initiations she verbally expressed her amazement at the energy she had experienced. Afterwards when we practiced hands-on-healing, she was astonished at the heat that came out of her hands. The people whom she worked upon praised her healing abilities. During one of the meditations during Reiki Mastership she had to sit out because she had experienced too much energy. She praised my teaching and brought me small unexpected gifts. Then about a month after the last class, she sent me a letter with the news that she wasn't a Reiki Master, that I was a fake, and that she was helping the community out by Xeroxing and distributing copies of a letter that she had received from another Reiki Master, who claimed that I was a fraud. Thank you! My students stood by me, the only one who didn't was Judas' friend. The thought that crossed my mind at the time was, "Jesus only had to contend with one Judas, so why did Mother-Father God feel it was necessary to send me two?"

Many of my students had taken my class so that they could teach. While they called me saying that they had felt the energy pass to them, and that they as well as their own students were satisfied, I felt that they deserved more. So, I asked Mother-Father God for the Truth. It is an interesting fact that much in our lives is dependent upon asking the right questions. So for this I will always be grateful to these two women. What initially could have been a disaster, became the impetus to alter my life forever. My prayer was heard and answered.

Shortly after Judas' relentless campaign began, an interesting series of events occurred. My Reiki Master, Margarette Shelton, was starting her last semester of graduate school, her father was dying, and she detested written correspondence. On that note she informed me on the

11

telephone that while she had documentation proving that I was a Reiki Master, I would have to wait for it. Secondly, I had written to the Reiki Master who had declared me to be a fraud, and asked him to further clarify comments he had made. When I received his written reply, I was amazed to find numerous contradictions from the initial letter that he had sent to Judas. In fact, he had even gone so far as to change his complete story. Eventually I ended up with 3 different letters, each with its own unique set of facts and circumstances. Thirdly, I was invited to speak and give a workshop that November at the Whole Life Expo in New York City, in the company of people I had seen on television and whose books I had read. In 1992 I had the opportunity to ask the director why out of all possible Reiki Masters he had asked me to be a presenter. He responded by telling me that he intuitively scanned all of the applications. I responded by telling him that I hadn't sent in an application; I hadn't even known at the time that the Whole Life Expo existed. He didn't have an answer.

When I arrived in New York, I stayed with a friend of Marcy Miller's, Charlotte Liss. Marcy had taken Reiki Mastership with me in Michigan. Even though I had been given a time slot of late Friday afternoon, a time when everyone in New York is still busy working, I lectured to a full audience and followed it with a packed workshop. As I drew in so many people, the Whole Life Expo asked me to be a presenter at the Los Angeles Whole Life Expo in February, 1991.

When I returned home to Milwaukee, Marcy called to find out how the New York Whole Life Expo had gone, and inquired about her friend, and now my new friend, Charlotte. Marcy also shared with me something very interesting. She had just been with a channeler in Arizona. While channeling she told Marcy that a woman named Kathleen had taken Reiki to higher levels. Being the only Kathleen Marcy knew, she then made immediate arrangements to fly from California to Milwaukee in December (something most Californians would not do) to retake Reiki Mastership with me. During the class I was struck with the realization that it was the exercises in the Runes and Egyptian Cartouche which raised the energy, and also awakened former lifetimes I had spent in Egyptian temples.

Marcy paid me for the class, but she was a guest in my home, as were all who traveled long distances to take my classes. Before she left, she wanted to return my hospitality and invited me to stay in Los Angeles with her after the Whole Life Expo there in February. When she left my home, she left for India to see Satya Sai Baba. Since his birth on November 23, 1926 Sai Baba has manifested supernormal powers and his mission in one phrase might be, to raise humanity's consciousness to God Consciousness. While he never went beyond the first grade, Sai Baba is able to communicate in languages he has never studied, and quote passages from texts he himself

12

has never read, at least not in this lifetime. His healings and manifestations can be imminent and dramatic. He is able to perform the same miracles that the Master Jesus did: Manifest, heal, transform, bilocate and even multilocate. There are countless stories and many books written about him, two by western medical doctors. When Marcy left my home, I wished her well and told her that I was looking forward to hearing about her trip and visit with Sai Baba.

The next time I saw Marcy was at the exhibition hall of the Whole Life Expo. While in India Sai Baba had told her in meditation that Takata had left out a symbol and over half of the initiation procedure for each of the three Reiki degrees. Smiling, she told me not to worry. Sai Baba had gone to the inner planes for the purpose of retrieving the lost information and power Dr. Usui had originally discovered, and that he would be giving us the information shortly. In the city of angels at the Sita Ashram where Marcy was staying, Sai Baba appeared etherically. The missing symbol Satya Sai Baba retrieved contained within it the symbol for infinity, a symbol that I had seen repeatedly in many different ways and from many different people at the Expo.

On the beach the following day, Sai Baba reviewed the initiation procedures and I was told to call the missing symbol Zonar. I was to reinitiate Marcy, and she me. I had decided that when I returned home I would reinitiate all of my students and teach them the full initiation procedures. Sai Baba, reading my thoughts, asked me how much I intended to charge them for this service. My response was, that I would give it freely. Rather than being rewarded for my spirituality and humility, he admonished me for not honoring myself. I then cautiously asked him if charging $10 would be all right. I held my breath, and to my great relief, he responded that that would be fine.

So for the sum of ten American dollars, the cost of lunch at a relatively nice American restaurant, I reinitiated and taught my interested students. Then I would have them "practice" on me. In this way the energy was built up. Everyone felt the increase in energy both during the initiation, and afterwards pouring out of their hands. Several people broke out in tears, crying this is it. I even reinitiated Reiki Masters from other associations, and they felt the increase in healing energy. As I moved upwards, those whom I had reinitiated moved up right behind me. When the process had been completed, however, we still were unable to do the same things that Mikao Usui and Takata could do. What else could be missing? Again I was heard.

April 1991 I found myself once again in New York. While sitting in Charlotte's New York apartment with a group of my students I mentioned that I was going back to California to teach a class in May, and that I would also be seeing Marcy. Coleen Zurawski and several other psychics present told me that Sai Baba and the masters had more in store for me. I gasped, how in the world was I going to explain this one?

I did not "fly over" the Midwest between visits to New York and Los Angeles, rather I went home. While in Milwaukee, one of my Reiki Master students, Rosemary Schoenenburger, casually informed me that I had something for her. When I asked her what it was that she thought I had, she replied, "A symbol with a cross in the middle of it." I did not have one to give her, at least not yet.

In May 1991, in California I again met with Marcy and Sai Baba. I was not completely taken by surprise when I was informed that it was the masters' intention to replace Zonar with Harth for the purpose of raising the Reiki vibration. I watched while the symbol was being drawn, the first lines were those of a cross. When the symbol was completed the cross was in the middle of a pyramid. Several years later, one of my students from New Jersey, Aaron Sapiro, told me that he had met a man whose family had left Japan just prior to World War II. As a young boy his family had done some work with Mikao Usui's Reiki Masters. One of the tools they had been given a half century ago was the symbol of a pyramid with a cross in the middle.

Everything happened just as before. Under the supervision of Sai Baba and other higher beings, we reinitiated one another. Again for ten dollars I reinitiated students and shared the symbol the masters called Harth. Each person I reinitiated felt the increase. Again after processing the energy we were able to do more for those who sought help from us, but we were not able to do the same consistent miracles that Usui and Takata were capable of. Hesitantly, I asked, "Why?"

Other Rays of Elemental Healing

From the first time Sai Baba, the masters and angels had asked me to speak out about the empowerment they had given me, I knew that it would create a stir. My personality would have been more content not to do this. I would have preferred to ride my horse and paint for the rest of my life. These guides, however, as early as 1991 directed me to include the fact that I was working with Sai Baba in the biographies I used in the programs where I lectured and in other promotional material.

After my lectures I gave time for questions, and invariably I would always be asked about my work with Sai Baba on the inner planes. I would answer to the best of my abilities and if I didn't know any answer, that would be my answer. Afterwards I would have a volunteer from the audience come up and I would give a demonstration of the healing energy. My guides and angels were always there and without fail Sai Baba would show up. People who saw on other planes always saw him.

At these demonstrations I would let the healing energy speak for itself. I put myself on the line and trusted that they would be with me. Shortly after this all began, I found myself in Chicago demonstrating on a woman after the lecture I had just given. As I was moved to place my hands on her neck, she suddenly flipped into a past life where she had been hung. Her neck elongated, her face became puffy and her eyes looked like they were going to pop under her closed eyelids. I moved my hands to her shoulders so that the audience would not think that I was strangling the woman. However, that seemed to be my concern, not theirs. During the course of her release and healing, everyone in the audience received a major healing in some part of their body.

This was the beginning, my guides told me that there was more to come. They chose to work with me at a slow steady pace. This allowed my spiritual teachers to see how I used the energy and knowledge they imparted to me. They also did not wish to overwhelm me, which is one reason all of us are fed time moment by moment. I can't imagine what I would have done if they had suddenly told me that they wanted me to write a book, produce video and audio tapes on healing, and establish an academy for the healing arts because there were other elemental rays of healing? Oh, and let's not forget the Egyptian hieroglyphs, the seven rays and color!

While I was in California with Marcy in February of 1991, we went to several group Light channeling sessions conducted by a former 'yuppie' (there are many of them in California). At such a gathering a psychic goes into a trance state. Rather than having a spirit speaking through the medium, s/he holds the doorway for healing energy from higher realms to come through so that those present benefit. Attendees can receive healing, and many choose to take advantage of the energy by entering deeper states of consciousness to maximize the benefits. An everyday example of this channeling of Light phenomenon is during the consecration of the host within a mass or service. The priest or minister (and some of them are conscious of what it is that they are doing) brings down the body of Wholeness, the Light of Christ Consciousness, into the bread. This is the body that Jesus referred to; the fact that we are all one, we all belong to the same Wholeness. Jesus was called the Christ because he had direct access to Absolute Consciousness. The more Light energy a psychic channel is able to draw in, hold, and radiate for the group, the more that can be accomplished by the individual participants. The sessions I attended in California were indeed powerful. When I left California for Milwaukee I was grateful for the experience and for the Reiki information Sai Baba had retrieved.

After returning home, one of my friends told me about a psychic surgeon who was teaching a class the following week. Unable to attend the training I scheduled a healing appointment with him instead. In the session he worked with the angels in a powder blue color that was strangely familiar. I asked, "What is this?" To my surprise, I experienced a knock on my head, and my guide, Straight Arrow, said, "Remember the Light sessions in California!" I looked to my dreams for the answer.

It is possible to problem solve in the dreamstate. This has been common practice for many very famous scientists, mathematicians, leaders and intellectuals through the ages, including Albret Einstein and Thomas Alva Edison. It is easy to do, and if it this effective we should probably be teaching this to our children. Just prior to falling asleep I write down all aspects of my question. Then I narrow down what I desire to know to a rhyme, a brief statement or a question. Short poetry works particularly well. I repeat the phrase over and over again until I fall asleep. The answer is then received upon waking the next morning either by an unmistakable inner knowing, or by analyzing all aspects of my dream. Immediately after opening my eyes I write down everything I remember - colors, locations, circumstances, objects, people, animals, what was said - everything. There are dream analysis books that are very helpful and if you are using one, your subconscious will provide the appropriate symbology. However, we are the best interpreter of our dreamscape metaphors. Within the imagery of our dreams lies the answer; and interestingly enough, there is often more than one answer or levels of interpretation. Sometimes this process needs to be repeated several nights in a row. Some people set their alarm clocks so that they can awaken at four o'clock in the morning and then they begin writing, or speaking into a voice activated recorder.

I asked about the connection between the Light sessions and the psychic surgeon. This is the message I received, "Each of the two men is working on the outskirts of something larger." Shortly thereafter I was told to call the powder blue ray Angeliclight.

In June, 1991 I returned again to California to teach another Reiki class. A woman who called herself a Seichem Master asked me if I would do an exchange with her for Reiki Mastership. I agreed, and I found myself channeling a different kind of energy from Reiki as a Seichem Master. Rather than energy running hot and cold as Reiki does, Seichem sparkled through my hands like effervescent bubbles or small electrical impulses.

The Seichem initiations were lacking in several areas, yet Seichem healing facilitators were able to initiate healing with this energy. When I was shown the Seichem symbols, I saw that they were identical to the Reiki symbols only slanted. Even the master symbol, the *Dai Koo Mio*, which is used to fully open the initiate to the Seichem healing ray, was the same as the Reiki *Dai Koo Mio.* What really caught my eye was a symbol that Sai Baba had told me that Takata had made up. Sai Baba told me that *Hon Sha Za Sho Nen* was a combination of Hawaiian shamanism and Buddhism. Sai Baba had proven himself correct so many times before I had to ask, "So if Takata had made up *Hon Sha Za Sho Nen,* what is it doing among the Seichem symbols?"

My answer came the following morning as clear as a bell and took me by complete surprise. In my dreams the masters and angels told me that Seichem played on the outskirts of a larger ray which in full manifestation comes in like a sparkling rainbow of color. I was told to call this energy Sakara. Later a Seichem practitioner told me that the individual who rediscover Seichem found it by reading the original Sutras, the same Sutras that Mikao Usui had read. It is my personal feeling that this particular individual came into conscious awareness and connected with this ray and its healing properties as they were reading the Sutras. More than likely, this individual had worked with this energy in another lifetime. However, what this individual did not do was to seek a conscious raising journey. Thus, neither the complete knowledge, nor the correct symbols, nor the full power was retrieved. Perhaps the world was not yet ready.

When I returned to Milwaukee I was approached by an array of 5th dimensional beings: the ascended masters, the Galactic Federation, and the angels of The Eternal Light. It was their intention, with my approval, to move me upwards from being a Seichem Master to a Sakara Master and at the same time initiate me into Angeliclight. They were serious.

17

This process took form through several methods. Meditation, visiting places of power and performing magic on a regular basis on the full and new moons were all a part of it. However, it was during an astrology reading that Larry Peterson gave me when I truly began to understand the depths of my involvement. Larry started by telling me, "You traveled a lot during the eight years prior to your becoming a Reiki Master." I answered, "No I didn't." He said, "Well then you moved a lot during those eight years." I said, "No, I've lived in the same home for eleven years." Deeply agitated he responded, "These aspects are too strong. You had to have traveled or moved around a lot!" Larry Peterson is very good at reading astrological charts, and one reason why he is so good is because he consults with the masters and his guides. When he did so about the confusion in my chart, they told him that masters, angels, Sai Baba, his teacher, Babaji, and others during those eight years had taken me out of body at night to other planets, solar systems and even to other universes to teach me the Sacred Mysteries and Laws of healing. From the time I became a Reiki Master, I have been in a process of remembering what I was taught.

Larry's insight made a great deal of sense to me. Before I ever heard that there were different Reiki associations in serious conflict with one another, before I had spoken in New York, when I taught Reiki I felt that the energy needed to be raised. I had done a series of oil-on-canvas paintings on the Holy Kabbalah and before teaching a Reiki class I would stand them on the floor along the walls and even in front of the windows of my living room creating a ring of energy. Within this vibration I would initiate my students and teach them Reiki. Also, during each one of the Reiki initiations I had been given, I kept waiting for something else to happen. I receive the first two Reiki degrees from Helen Borth, and after one of the initiations I remember asking her, "Are you sure this is all there is?" She just looked at me.

From my working with Sai Baba, other masters and celestial angels, my understanding and experience is that Reiki comes from the element earth, and the energy of this ray runs hot and cold just like surface of our planet. With Sai Baba's reintroduction of the full initiation procedures into Reiki, the color of the attunement as well as the energy that flows from the healer's hands changed immediately from purple to gold. When Mantak Chia found this out he called me from New York and made arrangements with me to reinitiate him as a Reiki Master. He felt that the Reiki Mastership initiation was the initiation of the Taoist Masters; he is a Taoist Master and he wanted his full initiation.

Earth energy is referred to by the Masters as Tera-Mai, my earth. An interesting point is that while traditionally a variety of hand positions are taught in the first Reiki class, the most effective hand placements are those where the hands lie parallel to the earth. Other characteristics of earth energy are those of grounding and foundation. Because of these properties, Reiki is fundamental to all of the other elemental healing rays. Without Reiki or grounding very little, or nothing else happens on the 'physical' plane. This is why Dr. Chujiro Hayashi gave Takata the symbols for elemental earth healing. In Japan 100 years ago men referred to themselves as Reiki Masters because they had command over all of the elements, the same four elements that comprise our own physical bodies. Today what we know of as Reiki refers to the healing ray within elemental earth alone.

Sakara is fire. Fire itself is a phenomenon that cannot be explained or defined by any scientist alive on earth today. This is because fire comes from the fourth dimension and lightening comes from the fifth. In our present physical forms we live on the third dimension. It is virtually impossible to explain fourth and fifth dimensional phenomenon using limited three dimensional terminology. What the masters told me was that Sakara or fire at the healing level is the vessel or vehicle which holds Angeliclight, the healing aspect of air. Sakara brings a rainbow of protective light which surrounds the aura. It is this merkaba or body of light which holds Angeliclight. This merkaba also allows one to astral travel into the higher realms, as opposed to out-of-body explorations of the physical universe, which is itself a variation of the physical trance state. True reality is the consciousness our soul experiences as Oneness.

In healing Sakara works in the aura, the electromagnetic field surrounding the body. One of the properties of fire is transformation. Sakara burns through and transforms blockages and resistances in the physical, mental emotional and other spiritual bodies. As they initiated me into higher levels of Sakara, low voltage electricity and later, what seemed to be lightening, both aspects of fire, moved through me. Even clients I worked on would use the words electricity and lightening to describe what was occurring in their body.

Later I was to discover that Sakara further aids in pranic healing, and balances the electrical-magnetic field. Prana is the vital Universal energy that surrounds us and sustains life. In pranic healing one uses what the Taoists would call Chi to clean the electromagnetic field or aura, the chakras and meridians. After the healer cleans the chakras, s/he then projects prana or Chi and healing colors to the client.

Typically we bring in energy through our left hand and foot and out our right hand and foot. When people talk about their "receiving hand," they are referring to their left hand; when they refer to their "sending hand," they mean their right hand. Using Sakara in the aura above the body we can reverse the flow by bringing healing energy in through the client's right foot and

19

hand, across each chakra, and out the left. The effect is as if we were to suddenly reverse a river; that is, debris that has been neatly tucked and filed away can be loosened and released.

Auras contain layers of electromagnetic energy fields, commonly referred to as the subtle bodies,which directly correspond to each one of the **major chakras**. In east Indian mysticism chakra means wheel. They teach that these chakras whirl outwards both clockwise and counterclockwise from the vertical energy line located within the physical body. This vertical energy line comes from Source, moves into our crowns and out our root chakras and grounds us firmly and deeply to the earth. The crown chakra spirals up, the root chakra at the base of the spine spins down. From this vertical energy line the other chakras spin out front and back into the aura. The clockwise spin draws prana or Chi into the physical body It is the counterclockwise motion that releases spent or misqualified energy. However, in healing sessions if you dowse with a pendulum over each chakra, the movement of the pendulum over a healthy chakra will be clockwise. This movement should be a balanced circle; neither an oval nor a straight line. If the major chakras are in harmony, the circles will be the same size. If measuring the navel chakra and the chakra at the small of the back, which is called the meng ming and also the door of life, these two chakras will be about 2/3's the size of the 7 major chakras.

The physical body is the last to express disease or misqualified energy. In aura healing two things are possible: Thought patterns in the aura can be released before they enter the physical; or thought patterns behind pain in the physical can be found, released and transformed in the aura. Working in the aura is one way in which the healing facilitator is able to bypass the ego, which is masking the root cause of the issue with physical pain. This is not to say that the physical pain or disease is not serving an important service. It is calling attention, and often rather loudly, to the fact that there is misqualified energy. That is, that there is a thought form or emotion being held that requires healing, transformation and release. Dr. Deepak Chopra, Dr. Bernard Siegal and other qualified medical doctors have been trying to tell us for years that drugs or surgical techniques alone serve only to mask the symptoms. If the root cause is not addressed, the patient is not healed. There is no monetary incentive for a doctor to prescribe herbs and homeopathic remedies. Ralph Nader's group has a book out available through his organization that was researched and written by medical doctors. Worst Pills Best Pills lists roughly 100 pills that should never be taken and about 700 deadly drug combinations.

Changes in the **aura** will be reflected by corresponding changes in the physical body. Physical transformation may or may not manifest immediately, but will be evidenced at sometime if the core issues are resolved.   Altering the energy pattern of the electromagnetic field causes repercussions which will be experienced on all levels.   Much healing work can be done in the aura, and there will be a time in the near future when healing energy will be able to reconstruct missing limbs and organs. Salamanders have the ability to regenerate; Salamanders also have a more active electromagnetic aura than other creatures. Interestingly, the Greek word for a fire elemental is salamander.

In the aura the root chakra and throat chakras correspond to the first and fifth electromagnetic fields These etheric bodies are associated with the physical body. The second or creative chakra, and the third eye correspond to the second and sixth fields. They deal with the emotional body. The solar plexus and the crown chakras relate to the third and seventh fields. These are the mental bodies. The heart chakra and corresponding fourth subtle body acts as the fulcrum. It is the entrance to higher levels of physical, emotional and mental expression. Without heart love energy, the passageway to the higher chakras is blocked. Without heart love energy, there is no compassion, the ability to see divinity in All There Is. Higher chakras are our gateway to knowledge of the Truth of Oneness because when heart love energy is directed to the upper chakras, our psychic centers begin to open.

As I mentioned previously, if you dowse a chakra with your pendulum, it should move in a clockwise circle. Most people measure the chakras just above the physical body, which is the astral body and is associated with the root chakra. Sue Szymanski moves the pendulum straight up through the aura over each chakra and in this manner measures the astral, the emotional, and mental bodies. For example, I once demonstrated this phenomenon on a woman who used her will center (solar plexus - first mental body) to extremes. As the webbing (necessary, protective weaving and interweaving of energy lines) in the solar plexus was worn thin, the pendulum moved in a straight line over that chakra. In addition the pendulum also moved in a straight line through the mental body of each one of the other major chakras. In this particular woman's case the pendulum not only moved in a straight line, but to the amazement of everyone watching, it arched higher than my fingertips which were quietly holding the chain.

Each major chakra is also associated with one of the major glands. If there is a problem in a gland, it will be reflected in the corresponding chakra. As the physical is the last body to manifest a misqualified thought form, it is possible to use Sakara to remove a blockage before it takes physical form. As I work my hands through the aura, the electrical impulses in my palms and fingertips literally 'zap' or transmute thought forms that are like hard stones. Once at Ishpiming I was working on a man, who felt that he was possessed. Just to the left of his head I found a dark, heavy area about 3 feet in diameter. I was aware of this form for only a moment, for it suddenly exploded in my hands. The man, who had been lying calmly on the massage table, jerked up and doubled completely over. He lay sweating with his head on his knees for fifteen minutes. In this individual's case the possession was gone, but he still had other issues that he needed to work out. All healers who work effectively in the human aura are working with Sakara energy whether they call it that or not.

There is another chakra at the navel, and a potential relationship exists between the navel, heart and third eye chakras; that is, the manifestation of the Holy Trinity within our earthly bodies. It is like this, there is a knowing that is felt in the heart, and there is a knowing in the visions we see with our third eye; we are supposed to be using them both together. We use all three chakras when we pray with our hearts, then wait for the visual answer in our third eye, and then ground the energy with the navel. In addition there are minor chakras throughout the body and in the palms of the hands, and the soles of the feet. The palm chakras of a healer will be developed, and they automatically become larger with the laying on of hands.

One of the greatest benefits to working with Sakara energy comes immediately after an accident. At this time the aura is literally shattered. Misqualified energy has surfaced at this time and will not solidify until three days afterwards. Within this three day time frame energy patterns are easily transformed and pulled out of the aura by using the pain drain (left hand over the area, right fingertips pointing down to the central fire). Then the healer's hands work back and forth through the aura to reestablish the healthy electromagnetic energy pattern in the aura. As the root cause is transmuted, sudden and dramatic healings can and do occur in the physical.

My friend, Marcy Miller, had flown in from California and was helping me paint the rooms of my home. Somehow I foolishly managed to fall off the ladder and sprain my ankle. She worked on it, drained off misqualified energy and put in beneficial energy. Healing energy can be put into the aura and body as the healer lays his/her hands over or on the area. Some people like to hold the palm of their left hand up in a receiving position, and radiate energy out their right hand. The flow of energy can increase if the wrists and elbows are unbent, and the arms are away from the body, which opens the chakras under the armpit. In less than an hour I was able to put weight on it, and the next day I was fine.

Because an accident shatters the aura, the other good news is that disease or pain unrelated to the accident itself, is also easily transformed. The problem may even be located in an entirely different area of the body. The bad news about an accident is that after three days, the

22

misqualified energy does take form. Time etches in undesirable energy patterns. The more time that is involved, the deeper and more ingrained these patterns become. If physical healing is possible, at this point it involves a considerable effort both by the higher self of the client and Spirit working through the healer to get to the cause and transform the physical. If, however, the karma has been worked out by the individual and there is no dependency on the injury, healing can be instantaneous. At the Whole Life Expo in Los Angeles in September 1992, while doing a healing demonstration in front of a packed lecture hall., in less than 10 minutes Beverly K. Henson released an arthritic hump on her thoracic vertebrae. Here is her account:

"I am not sure what led me to attend Kathleen's lecture at the Whole Life Expo in Los Angeles, in September of 1992. But, it changed my whole life.

My husband and I were without a baby-sitter and had taken our eight-year-old son with us that Sunday morning. He promised to sit quietly while Kathleen spoke. He found her lecture very interesting and paid close attention.

On the other hand, the arthritic hump on the upper part of my spine was aching so badly, I could not concentrate on everything Kathleen was saying. It had been hurting constantly for the past several days. Walking around the Expo for two days, carrying my purse on my shoulder, had not helped the situation either.

When Kathleen asked for a volunteer to come up on stage, my hand shot up before I could give it a thought. She asked where my problem was and then put her hand on the spot. She could easily feel the hump. As she began to work in my aura, she asked what emotional problem I needed to deal with. I couldn't identify with this, simply because I had shoved it to the back of my mind.

She worked on pulling a very heavy plug from my crown chakra and said that I would begin to deal with the problem soon. She worked on me for maybe five to seven minutes. When she finished, she asked how I felt.

I put my hand on the hump and it had definitely gone down. It was tingling like your hand does after it goes to sleep. I looked at the audience and told them it had gone down.

Over the next few days, the hump continued to disappear. Every single time I bent to pick up something heavy, I expected it to hurt. It never did. Two days later, I was watching a TV show about a person going back in time and telling his father how much he loved him. I broke into uncontrollable tears. These were the tears I had held back since my father passed away two months earlier. This was the emotional problem that Kathleen had pulled the plug on, enabling me to deal with it."

Angels and ascended masters processed within my being the energies of Sakara and Angeliclight throughout the summer of 1991. Always varying the initiation process. Always present on my journey. Always there when I was in high states of meditation. On two such occasions my heart stopped beating totally. I was literally lying in a strangely silent body when a hand dropped easily into my chest to massage my heart until it resumed beating. My inner knowing always told me that everything would be fine. I trusted.

23

For some people the idea of another human being channeling healing energy is so outside of their thought constructs that they laugh, or even become angry. Despite my own reluctance, there is a driving urge within me to stay focused and complete the process I am immersed in. I have found that when spirit asks us to do something, it is different then when we ask for something. During the summer of 1991 my two children and myself were completely provided for as I became a Sakara Master, one who is capable of transferring the fire energy from Source to the initiate. All the while angels busily wove the energies of Angeliclight in my aura.

Angeliclight is a two-fold ray; working with both the element air and the angelic realm. Air expresses the qualities of communication. In healing the effectiveness of the third eye *(Comprised of a chakra at the forehead and another between the eyebrows, which is associated with the inward eye of the mind.)* and throat chakras are increased dramatically. Watching and serving as a witness with the third eye while the healing takes place strongly intensifies the healing energy. With Angeliclight the healing facilitator is able to work effectively with angels, Holy Spirit, and the client's higher self. Angeliclight acts like an angel magnet. The first client Madonna Peters worked on after she received these initiations told Madonna that she had never seen so many angels gathered in her whole life. As I was initiated into higher levels of Reiki, the heat from my hands increased; as I moved upwards in levels of Angeliclight, heat began radiating from my third eye and even my physical eyes which intensified as time went by.

The other aspect of communication is the voice or the power of the spoken word. Angeliclight enhances this quality which is why those initiated into Angeliclight must have disciplined minds and be conscious of their words. I can call upon the masters, light workers or angels to help me during the healing process; if however, I call them by name, the energy wave that they come in on is stronger. If I repeat their names 3 times, it helps to raise my vibration; their's is already raised. Within The Magician's Companion by Bill Whitcomb can be found the names of 12 archangels translated from the original Hebrew. They are: Advachiel, Ambriel, Amnitziel, Asmodel, Barachiel, Cambriel, Hamaliel, Hanael, Malchielael, Muriel, Verchiel and Zuriel. "iel" means, of God, and chanting their names sets up a spontaneous, high vibration that can be used in healing, meditation or white magic.

With Angeliclight, when the healer speaks about what is occurring during the healing process, the energy is magnified and the experience is intensified for the client. When the healing facilitator observes, "The angels are bringing you an herb specific to your need, breath in deeply," the client oftentimes smells it. This phenomenon is incredible proof of the existence of another reality beyond our ordinary 5 senses. Scents from other levels of reality can be subtle

24

or they can come in very strong. The difference between smelling aromas originating from the physical plane and those from other realities is this: When you breath in the scent of a rose, the smell is consistently with you as long as your nose is in proximity of the flower. When the smell comes from other realms; however, the healer or the client may catch a whiff here or there on the same inhale. The aroma is neither consistent, nor does it linger. Sometimes you smell it, sometimes you don't. Other times you can smell a sweet fragrance consistently, but only in one particular square foot of space in the room and in no other. This often indicates the presence of a master or archangel. In either case the aroma of the herb or flower goes about and does its work with the assistance of the angels and holy spirits.

People have many different definitions for angels. Some people consider angels to be any disincarnate being. Other people refer to angels as the higher self. An interesting definition for angels comes from Alice Bailey. In her material, which is the foundation of all metaphysical knowledge today, she speaks of a parallel universe to our own. The elementals take form in that Universe in what the Greeks call the Silfs of the air, the Gnomes of the earth, the Salamanders of the fire and the Undine of the water. These beings do not go through a reincarnation cycle, rather they evolve through an unfoldment process. That is, it is the ultimate goal of each elemental to learn and master the aspects of the other three elementals. So when a Silf masters the emotional and psychic qualities of water, s/he becomes a two-fold being. When an elemental masters three elements, they are a three-fold being. When all four elements are mastered, they become what we call angels. Stories of the elementals are found in Greek, Celtic, Oriental and Native American lore. They have been loved, misunderstood and feared. They are also used in elemental magic, and in healing. In helping us the elementals help themselves and their own universe. The masters refer to the ray of elemental healing emanating from Source through this parallel universe as Angeliclight.

All psychic surgeons in varying degrees work with the energy of Angeliclight. After being initiated into Angeliclight, celestial angels are able to project themselves over the healer. That is, in channeling the spirit enters the body of the psychic and the channeler leaves; with Angeliclight healing, the angels gently overshadow the healers body. In overlaying the angels are able to reach through the healing facilitator and into the body of the client without cutting the skin to initiate physical changes. The client may feel angelic hands moving within them, or organs being moved. There have been instances where people have experienced the sensation of cutting away of tumors or diseased tissue. These healings are looked upon as miracles because the common elemental phenomenon and structure of their universe is uncommon to our own.

25

There are 333 levels of Angeliclight which the healer can receive through initiation which are given along with the Sakara and Sophi-El initiations. The levels are for our point of reference on this 3-dimensional reality. After the last initiations into Angeliclight are given, the healing energy of air evolves upwards on its own as the healer uses it. There comes a point, however, when Angeliclight becomes out of balance with the other elemental healing rays, and it is then that the other elementals earth (Reiki), fire (Sakara) and water (Sophi-El) are pulled upwards so that they will be in balance. There is no end to Angeliclight!

All of the elemental healing rays emanate from Source or Mother-Father God and interface with one another. They work individually and in combination. For example, in the throat chakra, Angeliclight adds to the power of the spoken word. Sakara brings in the fire breath of the Holy Spirit. Reiki or Tera-Mai grounds the energy. Sophi-El brings in an emotional appeal.

Sophi-El is both gentle and persistent like the water from which it comes. *(Originally I did not have the name for this ray, and one of my students suggested that is be called Celestial Star Fire. Sophi-El was the name the masters gave to me later.)* The ray's color includes all of the various hues of silver, plus white, and the velvet black of the void. The Great Void or Great Mystery is black like the Universal womb from which the Light emerges. Without black there is no Light.

Sophi-El reaches deep within the emotional bodies to find the core, cause and effect of the disturbance. I have found that Sophi-El will help heal the deep rage and defuse the outrageous anger bottled up in the emotional bodies of child abusers, wife bashers and other molesters, who are 'negatively' stuck in their lower bodies or lower chakras. Battered women have been known to break their attraction to physical abuse through things like assertiveness training, where they begin to regain a sense of self-worth. Sage Oh'hne, the founder of Ishpiming (P. O. Box 340, Manitowish Waters, Wisconsin 54545) and author of <u>Our Journey Home, a Guide to Conscious Ascension,</u> recovered from both alcoholism and being a battered wife. However, there is nothing thus far in modern medicine to alter the abuser's conduct or consciousness.

Addictions, be they to food, sex, alcohol, drugs, etc., are a way to compensate for not allowing the full expression of joy into our lives. There is a place in the brain which, to the inward eye of my mind, is perceived as a small black ball. Often my clients can see this in their own brains as well when I ask them to look within. Sophi-El in combination with the other rays of healing can remove the spot and bring in energies of joy and the feeling that, "I deserve to be happy!"

Sophi-El also opens the heart to receive love and feel compassion. A woman once brought her boyfriend to me. He had Multiple Sclerosis, which Louise Hay says is caused by hardheadedness as well as hardheartedness. He was having a particularly bad day. Exhausted and experiencing great difficulty walking, we stayed outdoors. While seven other people watched and felt the energy, Sophi-El opened the "iron doors" of his heart. Within two hours his head was clear, he was walking normally and he had his energy back. I saw his girl friend several weeks later and asked how her friend was doing. She answered, "So, so." When I asked the angels why, I was told that his heart had opened, but not enough. While he was financially capable of giving me more than $9, he blocked the flow by not honoring the healing, and was too embarrassed to come back.

Sophi-El further aids healing by reestablishing the feminine-masculine balance. When you are born a woman, you have what we call 2/3's feminine and 1/3 masculine energy. It follows that men have 2/3's masculine and 1/3 feminine energy. We have many soul mates but only one twin flame. Our split-away has our other 1/3 - 2/3's balance. Being fully open to both masculine and feminine aspects is necessary in order to become a fully integrated personality. Our feminine side holds our creativity, nurturing, psychic and healing abilities. Our masculine side is the left-brained teacher, the consoler and the true warrior that protects us and all we have created.

In addition to emotional healing energy, Sophi-El enhances the healer's psychic awareness. The increase in intuitive abilities aids the healer in visualizing, hearing Holy Spirit, and receiving psychic impressions while s/he is working. Additional psychic insight comes only through doing the inner work, and it is only through our healed feminine nature that we have access to the Akasic Records, all memories and all experiences. The only question that is allowed of the Akasic screen in our inner mind is, "What is it I am to know?"

Sophi-El and the other rays of touch healing are here for us to utilize in healing and also to help develop our psychic awareness. This does not mean that we can avoid doing the inner work. Rays of healing are not a quick fix or a pill. They will bring up deep, buried issues. Righteous anger that was never expressed needs a constructive outlet. That is, anger is supposed to both protect us and move us to positive expression. For example, if I have a client who has even one event where they failed to speak up when someone unjustly criticized them, that unexpressed righteous anger has remained bottled up inside of their solar plexus.

Outrageous anger needs to be defused, righteous anger needs to be expressed in a constructive way. Andrew Vaachs would say that it is better to feel the righteous anger as long as we need to,

27

rather than keep it bottled up inside. At some point one needs to feel the anger, transform it and release it. One woman was able to release the resentment she felt towards her mother for the total lack of love, and the humiliation she experienced as a child when spirit pointed out to her that her mother's conduct is now and always has been inappropriate (mental illness). How could she hold her sick mother responsible? How could she reason with insanity, which has its own twisted truth? When she gave up her need for her mother to love her in the way that she wanted to be loved, when she stopped caring what her mother thought about her, she was able to heal and release her childhood issues. Understanding opens the heart. When we totally reject our parents, we reject the gifts on all levels they gave to us. When we blindly accept our parents, we take on their heavy baggage as well. When we heal our relationships with our parents, we heal ourselves. Healing ourselves is the best thing we can do for our own children.

Sophi-El will defuse outrageous anger if the individual is willing to let the Light into the dark corners of the soul where the monsters lie hidden. When all four elemental healing rays are used together, the 'negative' energy has nowhere to hide. Once we let Light and Love in, feel the emotional pain or shame, the monsters shrink and we heal our physical bodies. We can embrace ourselves and love ourselves for being human, just as Mother-Father God has always done. We need to look at lifetimes where we were the ones who did the killing and let the furies run rampant.

There are people who say that they will do anything to heal themselves, anything but look within that is. We look outside and see a world of chaos and blame God. When we can look within and unscramble our own misperceptions, then the world we create and live in mirrors back to us beauty and harmony. The greatest thing we can do to heal this planet is to heal ourselves.

Besides coming from the elemental forces, the rays themselves carry what we call feminine and masculine energies. Reiki or Tera-Mai (earth) and Sophi-El (water) are the feminine expressions of the Godhead. Sakara (fire) and Angeliclight (air) are the masculine. These forces are a theme in variation throughout this holographic universe. In a hologram all parts are in relationship to the whole. This is one of the ways in which Mother-Father God creates the nature of the cosmos.

Other planes of existence and the souls in these dimensions are also comprised of these same four elements. It is possible, therefore, to send elemental healing energy to disincarnate souls, people who are not presently in a physical body, if they are open to receiving and processing the healing energy. When we see these spirits on other dimensions, they appear to us to be ethereal and airy. They do not think of themselves in these terms! Being in the physical actually depends upon where you are. The difference between living on a three-dimensional planet and existing in higher realms, is that as one moves up in vibration, form becomes less dense and more flexible. Moving up in vibration and awareness is what we refer to as becoming enlightened. In this process we comprehend the paradox that we have both form and are formless. We are both individuals and a part of the circle of All There Is.

An additional ray works with the four elements on all planes and all realities. It is **Cahokia**. It is the combined force of elemental power, the three-fold ray of the alchemist. Its colors are cobalt blue, metallic silver and royal purple. Cahokia uses the nuclear, electrical and water components of creation to bring about transformation and manifestation. In some healings the diseased tissue will be numbed or frozen by this ray while the angels diligently work.

For people choosing to be healers through initiations, during and/or immediately after the energy transfer into Reiki or other rays of healing, there will be a noticeable change or experience that will be perceived by the initiate and will be evidenced by those whom s/he works on. In addition, during the initiation the energy of each elemental healing ray will be experienced differently. For most people, the awareness of healing energy coming into their crowns and emanating from their hands is a profoundly different experience. It is important to own the initiation afterwards and experience its effects. When I teach Reiki I, as soon as the class has been initiated, everyone has an opportunity to share what happened during the meditation and initiation. Verbalizing helps the left brain to remember what the right brain experienced, and helps to integrate the two hemispheres of the brain. Then we jump right into doing hands-on-healing. In experiencing first-hand what the healing energy can do, they learn for themselves the multi-dimensional aspects of dis-ease and the nature of healing and reality. The word work is found within the word workshop.

Elemental healing energies flow from Source, through the healer and into the physical, mental, and emotional bodies, as well as into the electromagnetic field that permeates and surrounds the physical. Universal healing energy alters the energy of the client and changes the manifestation of the mass. This healing energy works with many techniques, and I have had many different kinds of therapists, nurses and yes, doctors take my classes. The reason why doctors, who only work with allopathic medicine, are not more successful than they are, is because they focus their attention on the the chemical aspect of the human body, and mask the symptoms with drugs and surgery. Our bodies are electrical and mechanical as well. If we weren't electrical then the electrical machines they hook us up to in the hospitals to take readings with would not work. It is impossible to take an electrical reading from something that doesn't have an electrical charge! The elemental rays can transform and manifest in other ways besides individual healing work. They allow the healer to hold ceremony. This is done on other levels, not consciously, through the second or creative chakra. That is, if I am teaching a class or if I am holding a full moon ritual, my second chakra creates an energy pattern that supports the angels and spirit guides who are summoned to be of assistance to those in the class or group. The ability to hold ceremony is the reason why, when I give a demonstration on one member in the audience, many other people who are watching receive benefits of healing as well.

Mother-Father God has promised that the psychic powers found within the healing rays will not be misused in this age as they have in the past. Abuses of Sakara and the forcible manipulation of Sophi-El sank Atlantis and brought Egypt to her knees. Stories are also told in cultures around the world about jealous shaman using their powers to destroy another shaman whom their egos felt threatened by. Rune masters through the use of symbols would create and send harmful energy to those whom they perceived of as their competition. The tale of Aladdin has its roots in Atlantis where magicians used crystals in healing and magic. They easily entered and left crystals until physical reality became denser, then this became harder to do. One pair of dueling magicians tricked the second into going into a crystal by daring him to do so. Once inside, the first magician sealed the crystal so the second could not come out. Envy and utilizing power for the purpose of controlling others moves civilizations backwards. In each succeeding generation less and less knowledge and Universal power is available to hand down. Jealousy is always looking outside of itself rather than looking within. We are each supposed to be the star of our own life.

When I began processing the other rays of healing, I was told that the angels and masters were working with two other individuals on earth at that time to bring back the elemental healing energies and Angeliclight. I am not, nor could I be an anomaly. The masters said that these two individuals had different names for the energy, and simply that we were all at different levels of development. I do not know who these individuals are, where they are now, or if they are still involved in the process.

What I know to be true about myself is that ever since my first encounter with Sai Baba my life has been fundamentally and dramatically altered forever. Everyone is entitled to their opinion. For those people who say that I am not working with Sai Baba or another higher being on the inner planes, that would mean that Marcy and I retrieved the energy, missing symbols and attunement process. The energy speaks for itself. I am only giving credit to where credit is due.

My guides have asked me to move to Arizona where I have been asked to reestablish an academy for the healing arts. Many psychics have asked in meditation, and I invite you to do likewise, as to whether or not this is true. I have zero interest in becoming the 'grand head Reiki Master' or 'grand dragon Reiki Master' or whatever. The school belongs to earth and to God; my earthly authority is only to see that it is established. In this school knowledge will be taught and energy transferred in its pristine form. It is like the homeopathic doctors, who were all taught the same fundamental facts. Yet, if you were to go to two different doctors, you might find it difficult to believe that they graduated from the same school. What they each did was to take the knowledge and make it their own. However, they had to learn the basic foundation. One student wasn't given different or conflicting information from another student. So, too, with those individuals I have initiated into Sakara and other rays of touch healing. Each channels the same Universal energy and is taught the same information on healing, but each healer practices the healing arts in a way that is unique to them. Sakara and the other rays of touch healing will only be taught through the school by qualified instructors!

As a note of interest, allopathic medicine is a philosophy which sees the physician as intervening in the disease and death process by attempting to counteract the symptoms through surgery and medicine. It is referred to as modern medicine, which has also become big business. Homeopathic medicine utilizes herbs in either their natural form, or by a process which dilutes the natural substance down systematically with water. The herb that is chosen matches the symptoms of the disease, thus stimulating the body's natural immune system causing the body to actually heal itself. As herbs in their natural state have spiritual qualities (Everything comes from God!), the core of the problem is addressed as well.

The masters will not allow a Sakara war in the way that there is a Reiki war today. There are incredible extremes in not only what is taught and not taught in Reiki classes, but also major price variances. I have heard of some people paying almost $30,000 who are still trying to get Reiki Mastership; people paying $300 for Reiki I, II and III and receiving absolutely nothing in the bargain; and I have heard of people giving it away because they say it is "nothing." Amazingly, price does not determine either the quality, quantity or validity of the material presented or the energy that is transferred. However, it would be my best guess that for those who say that Reiki is nothing, nothing is what they are giving! If there is no honoring, then there is no energy and no initiation. For those who charge a love donation for the initiations, what the initiate receives is affected by their generosity. According to Universal Law, it has to.

Before I go to any teacher I look to see if they are doing what they say that they can do. Granted, there are people who are better teachers than they are doers. In either case I look to their students. <u>The bottom line is: Are their students able to do what the teacher says s/he can teach them to do?</u> Does the energy transfer hold? I can understand why the masters and angels want Sakara and the other rays to be taught from a central school. Anytime I thought that I could release my responsibility or do it my way, I was stopped immediately in my tracks.

Now the masters do not think in terms of better or worst; there are no judgements. The Reiki Sai Baba revealed to Marcy and myself is what it is! It is in fact the same information and empowerment that Dr. Usui rediscovered.   As is true with any system, what works works and what doesn't will not stand the test of time. For example, there were many Impressionist artists. Those whose work we still admire are those artists who touch our souls and express a quality of Universal Truth that goes beyond the mastery of form, composition and color. These artworks literally have the ability to move us into higher states of consciousness.   And so it is true with all the healing systems, including allopathic medicine, that are available today.

Those healing systems that prove to be beneficial work in various combinations for different healers and healees. For example, Janet Goodrich Ph.D (psychology) and author of <u>Natural Vision Improvement</u> and Deborah Banker M.D. both recommend eye exercises, meditation, palming (placing the palms of the hands over the eyes, **not pressing**) and slowly decreasing eye glass prescriptions with the help of an eye doctor to assist their patients move out of glasses. Janet Goodrich stresses healing the emotional and mental issues behind our eye difficulties; Deborah Banker utilizes aromatherapy (inhaling combined scents of eucalyptus, lavender and peppermint - it's strong!) to clear the cavities behind the eyes (it's also effective for all sinus cavities), and Chinese herbs. The healing ability of herbs in their natural and organic form has long been known. Bilberry helped U.S. pilots to see when flying night missions during World War II, and today many people owe their night vision improvement to Bilberry.

In addition, to see clearly we need to give ourselves permission to see the whole truth and feel safe when doing so. Advancing beyond our fears and also our suppressed anger are vital to the healing process. It has been my experience that hands-on-healing helps us to move through pain and disease to health and wellness in whatever modalities we choose to utilize in our own healing

Trigger Points and Healing

<u>We can only see who we are.</u> What we do not like, even hate and despise in others is where we need to begin our own healing. It is a difficult realization and a most uncomfortable process to go through. <u>Denial is far easier.</u> However, for those with the strength of heart to look within and ask, "What is this individual mirroring in me?" great change, release and transformation is possible. In this way we all serve as teachers to one another. It is incredibly difficult to admit that what we judge others so severely for is also within us. For example, one of my students came to visit me. After she repeatedly criticized and judged another woman's actions, I finally turned to her and asked, "What is it within you that Diane is reflecting back? We can only see who we are." She turned white and walked away from me. Standing in the middle of the street outside my home, she called me over and asked me to look down the road. "Who do you see?" She asked me. I answered, "Nobody!" She retorted, "That's exactly the number of teachers I have!"

When we go to a healer, they are able to accelerate our healing process through their love and caring, and by channeling Universal energy. When I am serving as facilitator, I talk with, pray to, and work with angels, saints and spiritual guides. I am there to facilitate the process, not to tell my client whether or not to divorce their spouse or move to Tibet. I encourage participation of the healees as they share what they are experiencing in their minds and bodies as the healing occurs. I may be guided to have my client ask their own angels, guides and the saints questions, or tell my client what I see and hear so that they might ask and discern for themselves the truth within. All psychic messages are interpreted through the mind of the clairvoyant. Limited vocabulary and restricted concepts will influence psychic messages received in any reading, be it in a channelling session, out-of-body experience, near death experience, over tea leaves or during a healing session. As healees we are the integral key to interpreting psychic impressions in our own healing process, and we do not have to 'buy into' anything that we are told. In fact we should be going within to discern the Truth for ourselves. In going within, on the other hand, we also have to ask if we are in denial or blocking the Truth.

As healees our higher or greater selves are actually in charge of the healing process. We bring up <u>which</u> core issues are ready to be healed. During the healing process or afterwards we may be guided to make changes in our lifestyles, or see other healing specialists such as colon therapists, reflexologists, massage therapists, herbologists, acupuncturists, ayurvedic doctors, etc. In this manner healing evolves through a process, and each soul takes its own course in its own time.

Sometimes instantaneous healings occur, as with Beverly Henson at the Los Angeles Whole Life Expo. More times than not, however, a series of actions unfold. And even with Beverly, what appeared to the audience as a sudden and dramatic physical healing was in fact the beginning of a process that lasted for over a month. During that time she faced the pain and tears of her father's death, and then went through a past life regression to deal with the core of the issue that had been within the arthritic hump on her thoracic vertebrae. For most people the emotional and mental issues heal first and then the physical body follows.

Layers of misqualified energy from many lifetimes come up for healing. We heal one issue, we feel good for a time and then something else comes up for healing. For many people total instantaneous healings would be too much of a shock, the process has to be gradual. How quickly or how gradually the process unfolds depends upon a great many factors. How ingrained is the 'negative' thought form? How many lifetimes has this thought pattern been repeated? How much work has the individual done on him/herself before coming in for a healing? How much energy is the healer able to channel? And is the healer focused and concentrating on the healee? In group sessions, the healees need to center their attention on the healer.

While healers are channels through which healing energy flows, there are techniques described throughout this book that can be utilized. Many healers pray for or invoke the help of angels, holy spirit guides, Jesus, Mary and other masters, as Mother-Father God chooses to work through them. People who do what is referred to as charismatic healing, work with the energy of the Holy Spirit. This energy comes directly from God (as does all healing energy), flows into their crown chakra , and out the palms of their hands; they are never sure when this will happen. Thus, to increase the healing energy, I can place the tip of my tongue on the roof of my mouth while I am in the process of doing hands-on-healing. Our breath is powerful; the soul enters the body of a newborn with the first breath and leaves the body with the last breath. I can use my own breath to blow away gray cloudy areas, and I can ask my client to breath away misqualified through their mouth and breath in beneficial energy through their nose.

Sometimes misqualified energy is psychically burned out in the body of my client, which they experience as a warmth within. If they are having difficulty releasing, I place my hand directly on the body where the pain or disease is and ask them to focus on the healing fire that is in the palm of my hand. I then ask them to will the pain or disease into my hand and allow the fire to burn and transform it. If my hand feels like ice to my client, I ask them to feel or envision the cold freezing the pain. When my client realizes that I personally am not taking on their 'stuff', it is easier for them to release and heal.

34

Other times misqualified energy is not burned, rather it leaves my client and begins to fill my hands. Because blockages have different energy patterns, their sensation is different. For example, cancer cells on the etheric level, for whatever reason, feel spongy. Pain can be electric, sharp or dull, and often I am able to describe my client's pain to them without actually being in pain myself. When this energy fills my hands, I literally grab it and <u>slowly</u> pull it off. I can then either throw it downwards (my intention being that it will go to the central core of fire, earth's inner sun) or lift it upwards (to the Light or to God) for transformation. Making counterclockwise circles with my hands helps release the unwanted energy patterns; however, sometimes a few clockwise circles in between helps to loosen the blocks.

Another method for releasing blockages works with electromagnetic energy and is actually the first step in becoming a psychic surgeon. I stretch my arms out straight and place the palms of my hands on my client. I visualize and feel myself becoming an electromagnet and see the blocks, like iron pellets, being drawn up into the arms of the magnet. I can also ask my client to visualize or feel this process; or ask them to will unwanted 'stuff' into the magnet. I then <u>slowly</u> lift my arms above my head. When I reach the 7th layer (corresponding to the 7th or crown chakra) I flip my hands over, which reverses the polarity of the magnet, and the misqualified energy is sent to the Light for transformation. I often repeat this process 2 more times. What do my client's think about my strange behavior? They are grateful. Alterations in etheric energy patterns at the foundation of the disease or pain initiate changes in the physical.

After the old patterns have been pulled off, I wash my hands and arms up to my elbows etherically. Sometimes I need to excuse myself and run my hands and arms under cold water, which breaks up any remaining vestiges of unwanted energy patterns. When blockages leave my clients, they often experience an emptiness where the misqualified energy had been. This void needs to be filled so that they do not draw back the same energy or something like it. This can be done simply by placing my hands on the body or in the aura and allowing the angels and other spirit helpers to fill the area with healing. If I focus above my crown and follow the vertical energy line upwards, I can contact the Universal rainbow of colors, which is available to everyone, and draw the healing colors into my crown, through me, and into my client. Angels and spirit guides always know what is needed. <u>Once the blockage is released, my client should not talk about the way they used to feel, or they will call the misqualified energy back to them by reweaving the old energy patterns</u>. When it's gone, it's gone and we need to let it be!

In a healing session sometimes people are not aware of what the blockage is that they are releasing. If they do not need to know, these individuals have worked out their karma and learned their lessons. Frankly, for them it does not matter whether or not the conscious mind is aware of it or not. As long as the lesson is learned by whatever conscious or subconscious aspect of the personality that needs to 'get it' does, physical healing can and will occur. However, if the disease is caused by a present mode of thinking, emotional pattern, or behavior then the individual needs to be made aware of what it is they are or are not doing. For example, there are people in this world whose utterances are more poisonous than a viper. Their words are like mosquitoes; they have a nasty sound, they are incessant, they sting and they leave behind a mean welt.   If no one has ever asked these individuals, in the moment these words are spoken, to listen to what they are saying, then it is up to the angels to guide the healing in such a way that they can see for themselves how harmful and hurtful their words are. How their words are not only injurious to others, but to themselves as well.

The 'bad movies', those haunting scenes from the past where we or others remain unforgiven, and those self-destructive 'audio tapes' we play in our heads can be released and transformed in the healing process. When we are able to forgive ourselves, then we can forgive anyone. At this point we are able to turn our attention to creating love and joy in our lives by substituting positive affirmations about ourselves, those attributes that our friends and relatives love and like about us. The reason why some actors and actresses become addicted to drugs and alcohol is because their positive affirmation is the final product; the movie, television show, play, etc., rather than all of the necessary qualities, abilities and personality traits it took to get them the part. It is the process that is the product! When we die, we take our experiences with us, which are far move valuable than a coffin filled with gold!

Oftentimes angels and spirit guides ask the healee to look past the mask of pain and disease to discover and accept what in them is creating the problem. This is not easy! However, it is in the total acceptance of self and the realization that Mother-Father God has always loved us, that issues can be transmuted, pain drained, and the body healed. We do not relish the idea that we are not only the actor/actress in our lives; but in addition we are every bit as much the screen writer, director and producer. We take solace in thinking of ourselves as victims, rather than seeing that we are co-creators of the events in our lives. When ego creates a world of denial, or our state of being is numbed out, our personal truth separates us from Universal Truth and Oneness. When we can clearly see how we are creating our 'negative' role, then we can call a halt to the game, and turn our attention to creating the best for ourselves. We need our egos but we need them to be in a healthy state of self-love and self-acceptance. It is in this state of mind that we are able to seek Wholeness, the sensation of our own blood dancing in the Light.

There are several ways in which we can discover the truth and reach behind the mask created by an ego that is in denial, distortion, omission, or inversion, which makes us see evil as good and good as evil. For example, there are many possible reasons for being overweight. 1) Eating has become a substitute for feeling and experiencing true joy: Are there undesirable, buried emotions? Are there issues that prevent us from fully participating in life's expression; for example, eating has become a substitute for a positive sexual relationship. 2) It doesn't matter what the individual eats or does not eat, patterning from another life time is influencing the present: Did the individual starve to death in another lifetime and because of this fear s/he is overcompensating in this lifetime? At the other end of the spectrum, I have one overweight student who knows that in another lifetime when he lived in China, the body weight he carried then was a reflection of his personal energy. The memory pattern in this lifetime manifests as an inability to properly digest food and as a result he gains weight. 3) Excess pounds can serve as protection: Before the companion videos to this book were finally produced, I put on 10 pounds that would not come off no matter what I did. These 10 pounds I believe protected me through a series of events that reached its peak the day of filming when the entire morning was spent fixing things that never should have gone wrong in the first place. The director told me that some of these events were a one in a million occurrence, and the fact that so many of these things were going wrong defied the laws of chance and probability. Just before lunch I did a clearing and invoked divine protection. No one seemed to mind. They were all grateful that I wasn't being a bitch about all of the delays. After clearing misqualified thought forms, shooting proceeded 'normally.' By seven o'clock that evening every camera person, every technician, the director, my son, Lee Owrey (who also had gained weight before the filming), and myself looked like we had come through a war zone. After the filming I lost the 10 pounds.

Fasting isn't necessarily good for loosing weight because it can throw our metabolisms off. However, fasting is one way to clear the body and bring up the emotion hiding behind the disease or the weight. Heal the emotional issues, and the pounds come off. There are many good fasts, each for a specific organ or gland, listed in Hanna Kroeger's book, Old Time Remedies for Modern Ailments. On the third day of a fast or cleansing, hunger comes up the strongest. If we eat, we feed the emotion; if we resist hunger and continue with the fast, the emotion comes up for healing. Some people find it beneficial to work with a professional, or healing facilitator while fasting. Spirit is then able to move the issue up quickly to be looked at, felt, released and transmuted.

True, many individuals have childhood and adolescent pain from this lifetime to heal. For most of us the wound goes back even further. Brian Weiss, M.D. has written books on reincarnation, the most familiar probably being <u>Many Lives Many Masters</u>. The greater majority of medical doctors who are presented with past life facts choose to ignore them, and not deal with the issue at all. In experiencing a past life regression, if we are with a trained therapist or qualified healer, when the unresolved issue or misunderstanding surfaces then the disease or pain is transformed, released and healed. The idea behind a past life regression is not to find out who we were, because it is vital to live in the moment. The reason for going through a past life is to heal the core issues.

When I initially heard about the concept of reincarnation, I immediately thought of God as being much more loving. How compassionate to give a soul more than one chance to 'get it right.' How appropriate for us to experience our thoughts and actions coming back to us in future lifetimes. However, this remained conceptual until I had the experience. Getting into a past life is not just watching a nice visual movie played in our brains, although all past lives are experienced through our brains. Getting into a past life is just that, we are literally feeling and living it.

My first experience with a past life came after I watched a series entitled <u>The Six Wives of Henry VIII</u>. Henry's first wife, who had been his older brother's wife, was very popular and nobody in England liked his second wife, Anne Boleyn. Nobody cried when she was beheaded. I didn't even like her. Shortly after the series I was in a place of no mind and no thoughts, simply making my bed. All of a sudden it felt like someone punched me in my solar plexus and I was struck with the knowing and the horror that I was Anne Boleyn. The feeling and the knowledge remained and would not go away. In fact, I knew things about Anne's life, like the fact that I had a lying and abusive brother, that I was an excellent horse rider, that I played a stringed musical instrument and had what was considered a lovely singing voice, and that my family was still secretly connected to Celtic magic. Queen Elizabeth I was known to have a healing touch. I even knew that I haunted the castle after my death, creating the illusion of carrying my head under my arm and frightening Henry. Within a week's time after spirit gave me the one-two punch I was at a party, and a psychic approached me. Apparently the trauma was so in my aura that she took one look at me and said, "You were Anne Boleyn, weren't you?" I, opened mouthed, could say nothing. She went on to say, "You have been carrying a burden of shame for hundreds of years. You didn't have to be beheaded in that lifetime, it was your own guilt that brought you to the executioner. Just think of it this way, you didn't ask Henry to marry you. Henry asked you to marry him." With that, the overwhelming self-hatred that I had carried since a small child was lifted from me. When I meet Henry VIII in this lifetime he was a Roman Catholic priest.

One of the things that remains active in this lifetime from my lifetime as Anne Boleyn is what I call 'the voice.' It has always been with me, and I never know when it will come out. I used to teach first grade at a Catholic school under my former married name, Kathleen Owrey. One Good Friday I was in church attending service. Several church members were playing modern renditions of old bible songs. As I walked down the aisle on my way to kiss the cross, all of a sudden I found myself belting out the melody with the boys in the band. For what seemed like forever, but in all likelihood was only a minute, everyone else stopped singing. It felt like my whole body was blushing.

Child prodigies bring in with them talent developed in other lifetimes. Many people have remembrances of past lives when they vacation or travel for business. However, when a misunderstanding, fear, etc. from a past life manifests in our current life, then we need to go back and heal the unresolved issue.

When I intentionally guide an individual through a past life regression, or if one comes up suddenly during a healing session, one of my first suggestions to my client is that they will be able to rise above their body at any time. They can simply detach and observe the process. In this way they need not re-experience any physical pain. When I close my eyes and go within, I journey with my client and their spirit guide or guardian angel. In this manner I am able to tell if their perceptions are superficial or on target I literally share their experiences, and the healing is similar to shamanic soul retrieval. The difference being that in soul retrieval work my client is in a nonactive meditation; while I am actively participating in a deep meditative state. In past life regressions they are visualizing, seeing, hearing and feeling; I am there guiding my client's experience. I do this by verbally giving them suggestions as to where to go or what to ask. Because I am with my client I am able to see when guilt and fear are causing denial. For example, one of my clients, Mary, reached the end of the tunnel *(which actually represents the birth canal)* and she saw herself as a woman in ancient Egypt. As we walked into the pyramid she saw a craftsman and said, "I don't understand this, at the bottom of the tunnel I saw myself as a woman and now I see myself as a man. Who am I?" I asked, "Who are you?" Mary said, "I want to be the artisan." I responded, "Ask your guardian angel who you are." Her guardian angel told her that she was the woman. There was a confusion because she didn't want to see who she really was. It turned out that she was a high priestess *(in her present life she didn't even know that there was such a thing),* who was excessively cruel and abused her power. In two other lifetimes we visited, and also in her present lifetime Mary was and still is a 'victim.' Her karmic debt was to experience firsthand the misuse of power by another. Now that she understood why she played the victim roll and having learned her lesson, Mary was in a position to either leave her controlling husband; or if she decided to stay in the marriage, she knew that she didn't have to be subjugated to his will.

The reason why Mary had been unable to leave her husband in her current lifetime was because in one former lifetime we went to, she had been a badly battered woman. She had left her husband and took their 2 children to another town where she became a beggar. One of her children died shortly afterwards. Later a man took both her and her surviving child in. He ignored her child, who later ran away, and the man abused her. She died in shame, guilt and fear. Mary now understood why every time she had wanted to leave her present husband, a terrible, unknown fear would literally consume her. Somewhere in her subconscious was the memory that if she left her husband, things would only get worse. Now Mary was free to make a clear, unfearful decision as to whether to stay in her current marriage or get a divorce.

Once in the past life, in order to get my client to the particular moment where the misqualified thought form originated, I suggest that they go to an important day in their life. Their higher self knows what I mean and will get us to the right place and time. I then ask my client to describe what is going on. There also may be more than one misunderstanding in more than one lifetime, but the first one is usually the most important. Then I ask them if there is anything else that the angels want to show them. Typically the next step is to ask them to go to the last day of their life and observe the death process. They hover over their body and watch their soul leave the physical body with the last breath. The proces is empowering in itself, for once anyone sees and feels their personality surviving death, they never have to fear death again. Then they call in their angels and spirit guides. Depending on the situation, my questions go something like this: "What did you come into this lifetime to learn or experience?" "Where was there a misunderstanding?" "What and who needs to be healed?" I then use the healing energies and their own visualization and feeling process to resolve, transform and release the pain. If we have gone to other lifetimes I will ask, "How does this lifetime relate to the last lifetime? How are both of these lifetimes related to your current life?"

Sometimes a client comes to me with a specific request. Samuel Minond had told Charlotte that she needed to go back to one of her Egyptian lifetimes in order to meet the scribe of Isis. I had a feeling that this wasn't going to be easy. When we were going down the tunnel, one moment Charlotte was with me, the next moment she was nowhere to be found. I asked her where she was, and she replied, "I don't know." So I asked her to ask Chriss, her son who had passed away, where she was. Chriss said, "Ma, you're in Never Never Land." Good avoidance strategy, go to the land of Oz! After getting back on course and down and out the tunnel, we were in ancient

Egypt. The temples and monuments were very large in comparison to the human figure, so that man could keep him/herself in perspective with Mother-Father God. We found the scribe of Isis, who was angrily accusing her of a crime. Charlotte sniffed burning rubber, then she realized that she was smelling herself. Apparently she had been found guilty of stealing secret esoteric writings, and as a punishment she had been tarred and burned. Charlotte was horrified as old shame and guilt came up to be felt, released and transformed. She observed the death process from a distance and watched the soul rise out of the body. I asked her to consult with her spirit guides and angels and ask them, "What was my lesson in this lifetime?" She was told, "To listen to yourself." Apparently, someone else had asked her to steal the documents, and she had never questioned within as to whether or not it was appropriate for her to do so. By looking at the event from another angle, she could see her lesson, release the shame and horror, and heal.

Then the scribe took Charlotte to the Akasic Records, the Truth of all memories and events. I was then guided to help Charlotte find the screen to the Akasic Records in her inner laboratory. Charlotte's male guide, David, had always actively assisted her, while her female guide, Shoshanna, came in only for group hugs. Now it was Shoshanna who led Charlotte to this sacred well of wisdom. And we both came to the realization that the knowledge found within the Akasic Records is available only through our healed female sides. In order for us to acquire this portal into the Mind of Mother-Father God, we must be willing to do the inner work by looking at events and lifetimes where we abused power and forgot to love. We do this by letting Light and Love into all of the dark corners of our souls (we can even do this as a visualization in meditation), healing our issues and loving ourselves for being human. The only question that is allowed of the Akasic screen is, "What is it I am to know?"

In dealing with the emotional patterns of their clients, modern psychologists work with the inner child. From the time of the first trauma, or the day the youth began taking drugs, that child's emotional body stopped growing. Charlotte says that what psychology fails to do is to put the horror that the child experiences in perspective. If we are dealing with an inner child who is overwhelmed, the burden of shame is magnified in the child's eyes and looms toweringly overhead. By putting the guilt into perspective, it becomes at first manageable, and then healed and released.

Sometimes a client will flip into a past life during a healing session without being regressed. One gentleman, a former priest, objected dramatically to the possibility of past lives before he even came to me. He even asked me if it was necessary for him to believe in reincarnation in order for him to schedule an appointment to see me. I responded that it didn't matter to me

41

whether or not he believed in reincarnation. Then he asked me if I was going to try to talk him into believing in reincarnation. I answered, "No!" During the healing session suddenly he found himself dramatically experiencing another lifetime as a Mayan priest. In journeying through the temple we found souls held earthbound within a dark room. We were asked by the angels and spirit guides present with us to lead the lost souls into the Light. I also felt that there may very well have been an aspect of his soul that had been held in the temple.

Numerous people who have come to me for healings have flipped into past lives where they were burned alive as witches. Many times their reluctance to do psychic and healing work in this lifetime stems directly back to that experience where they died because of their beliefs. When the past life is healed, they no longer have to make fear-based decisions. The inner clutch is gone.

Sometimes a past life surfaces for a client after I get an impression. I was working on a woman at Ishpiming when I received the name, "Constantine." As there are relatively few 'famous people' in history, my left brain jumped in and said emphatically, "No!" "Constantine" came again. Feeling the power of the woman's spirit under my hands, my left brain conjured the possibility that perhaps this was one of Constantine's generals. The name Constantine persistently repeated, and I reluctantly spoke the name to my client. Her eyes opened like a shot. She was amazed that I had picked up what she had known for most of her life. Ever since she was three years old she had cried irrepressible tears at every new and every full moon. Thus far, she had found that Transcendental Meditation was the only method of controlling her uncontrolable remorse. From the time she could first remember, she carried within her heart what felt like a heavy object. This battle-weary warrior longed to return to the Light and trusted that I had released my own judgements and was channeling the healing energy she needed to heal. As past lives were being healed, during the session I pulled off many past life cloaks and garb which represented the shedding of and healing of old issues. Included in her etheric closet were many red hats as well as pontiff hats. However, there was one particular bishop's hat and the lifetime she led while wearing that hat that was too familiar to me. I realized that this man had had me burned alive as a witch and I could actually feel singeing smoke in my lungs. Her friend and one of my students, who were observing the process, later told me that my face went white when I saw the bishop's hat and they expected me to either start choking her, or throw her off of the table. Instead I helped her to release her guilt, and even explained to her that many ascended masters had lived lifetimes as warriors and even black magicians before they returned to the Light. As Constantine and the many past lives between then and now were healed, the smoke cleared out of my lungs. Because I put aside judgements and aided my 'enemy,' great healing came to me. Straight Arrow told me that I will never fully be conscious of the rewards bestowed upon me because of this single act of compassion. Your enemies may or may not come to you for healing or forgiveness; if they do, heaven will reward you too for your generosity of compassion.

We can all receive great gifts when we at the very least bless our enemies and send them away with love. In this manner we halt the games without getting into judgement. When we suspend our judgements and love people where they are, we give them permission to find their own way home. Who are we to say that another's path is wrong? When we stop judging others, we stop judging ourselves. Who is to say that we ourselves in another lifetime were not the inquisitors and burners of the innocent? Mother-Father God has always loved and forgiven us. It is up to us to love and forgive ourselves and embrace ourselves for being human. It is then that we can use both intellect and compassion to seek Wholeness.

Sometimes during past life regressions I utilize the opportunity to satisfy my own left-brained curiosity. The Illuminati or the Illumined Ones date directly back to Constantine. These are the 7 families that you keep hearing about, who own the greater majority of the world's wealth. They are the 7-headed beast in the Apocalypse. Larry Abraham says they call themselves the Illuminati because they think they know something that the rest of us do not know; that is, that there is no God. They also refer to themselves as the son's of Apollo. Peter De Rosa, a former priest who worked in the Vatican archives for years, wrote a book, The Vicars of Christ, The Dark Side of the Papacy. In this book he describes how Constantine was praying before a metal statue of Apollo, the sun god, the day before he and his men marched upon Rome. They did not have a chance of victory. Suddenly, Constantine saw black rays pouring out of the statue and he knew that his prayers had been answered. I asked my client, who was experiencing her past life as Constantine, about the incident. She told me that Constantine knew in the moment that the rays were evil and assumed that God was evil. It was not God that answered his prayers; Constantine only assumed that it was God. More likely it was Lucifer himself.

Another time while working with Charlotte in New York, she went back to a lifetime where she was a high priestess in the Temple of Isis. After I learned how to do Native American journey work with one of Michael Harner's teachers, Myron Eshowsky, I had the distinct impression that we had done journey work in the Egyptian temples. Shaman means, one who works in the dark. To help reach deep states of meditation and to be able to see clearly with the third eye, shaman often wear blindfolds while journeying. In exploring Charlotte's Egyptian past life I discovered that 'the veil of Isis' was the Shaman's blindfold. Journey work was as much an integral aspect of Egyptian metaphysical practice as it was with the witches or wise ones, and still is with indigenous people. We have not begun to fully comprehended either the use of, or the extent of this practice. Mary Magdalen was not a prostitute! Some church official along the way decided that she was the one that Jesus saved from stoning. Mary Magdalen was a priestess and one of Jesus' followers. When she comes to me she refers to herself as "Mary Magdalen of the veil."

Healing past lives are a means of healing the present, but people do not have to go through a past life to face the emotional issues behind the pain and disease. Rebirthing is another means of bringing emotions to the surface. The rebirthing breath is the breath of infants particularly during the birthing process. That is, there is no pause at either the bottom of the exhale or top of the inhale. Breathing is continuous. Rebirthing therapists guide their clients through the embryo stage in uterus, birthing and childhood. In this way the breath surfaces negative emotions that are experienced, released and healed. Sometimes people are simply guided on their own to do this breath during a hands-on healing session. Often this happens when a client has done rebirthing.

Rebirthers say that hope is for the hopeless; it is the last stage of hopelessness. Rather than Faith, Hope and Charity, rebirthers might see the three virtues as Faith, Trust and Charity. Hope is looking for a specific outcome; whereas Trust is allowing Mother-Father God to handle the details of our desires. In healing, both the healer and healee need to trust that God through holy spirits and the angels will bring up the issues that are ready to be healed and released, and along with it the corresponding healing of the body, mind and emotions. The nature of healing is such that the healer gets out of the way and allows the individual to heal or not to heal in their own way and in their own time. When we see for ourselves how well Mother-Father God orchestrates healing, we are then able to trust God in our lives.

There are many techniques that a healer can utilize. A woman named Eleanor Moore, who lived in the Eastern United States, healed emotional issues in this manner: When Eleanor Moore facilitated healings in a group setting, she would have one individual lie upon a table. Everyone else present touched, comforted and encouraged the healee. For example, everyone present might chant "Ohm" for a period of time. During the healing process if a pain or paralysis came up she would take note as to which side of the body it occurred on. If the discomfort was on the left side, the issue went back to a woman *(mother, sister or grandmother, etc.)* and Eleanor would have the client yell "Caw" *(like the sound that the crow makes)*. If it manifested on the right side, the issue went back to a man *(father, brother or grandfather, etc.)* and Eleanor would have her client yell "K" *(pronounced just like the letter K in the English alphabet)*. The words themselves carry no meaning, yet they allow unexpressed righteous anger and other emotions to be experienced and released so that healing transpires. What I tell my clients is this, "Your parent *(or perpetrator be s/he alive or dead)* is literally counting on you to yell out and express the buried rage in order to break the cycle of pain and negative experiences for you both."

A healer does not necessarily need a group to facilitate the Eleanore Moore process. I encourage my clients to participate in the healing process by sharing what is going on. If my client has a sudden pain or paralysis and I am inspired to use Eleanor Moore's method, I call upon her spirit to assist in the healing. I place my left hand on the solar plexus and my right hand on the heart chakra. Depending upon which side of their body holds the pain or paralysis, I have them yell "K" or "caw" at their perpetrator. I have had clients who have had one whole side of their body become suddenly paralyzed; dramatically revealing how constricting and debilitating 'negative' emotions can bind us. At this point I reassure the healee that something has come up to be healed and that they will regain normal movement after they start yelling "K" or "caw," and they always do.

Sometimes people, who think that they have an issue with one parent, actually are angry with the other. For example, I have had women who were sexually abused by their father as children, yet the pain or paralysis comes up on the left side. These particular women were mad at their mothers for saying nothing and allowing their fathers to rape and molest them. One of my clients in about an hour's time went from her left side (physically beaten by her mother), to her right side (sexually abused by her grandfather), and back to her left side (mentally and emotionally abused by her grandmother). In any of these cases the healer can place his/her hand on the throat and massage gently upwards to aid in the releasing process. Depending upon the circumstances, to further encourage release, I might say, "This is a yell?" or "See your (perpetrator) doing something to you or saying something you hated them for. Feel your anger. Now yell at them."

When the client has had enough, their throat will become sore. It may become sore after only yelling a few times or even once, and is an indication that it is time to stop and breath in Light and Love from Mother-Father God. In this healing modality it is not the yelling that makes the throat sore but rather the emotion that is finally being expressed. When the emotion is released and healed, the pain, disease or paralysis is also released and healed.

Unexpressed, unfelt anger manifests as dysfunctional behavior. For some the rage is so deep, that they are afraid to bring it up. The following method works for many people in such a position, and again is a safe way to voice the fury. I ask my client if they would be willing to have the angels bring into their third eye (<u>their inner vision</u>) the people whom they are incensed at. One at a time, they are to then vent their rage however they wish to do it, submachine gun, shark, or axe the form. I tell my client that they are not killing these people or harming their souls in anyway. <u>The individuals, the forms the angels bring in only represent unexpressed anger</u>. **<u>The healee is killing off childhood misperceptions, fears and attitudes that stay with us and distort and 'mess up' our whole lives</u>**. Quite literally the people who are brought into the inner mind are counting on the healee to break up the rage and call a halt to the downward cycle.

For example, Connie began with her cold-hearted mother whose form immediately turned to stone. Connie and the angels dynamited her mother! Connie, to her amazement, felt a release of anger. She brought in her father. His form was a thick mucus-like substance that had a foul stench. She torched him! Again she felt a release. Connie was surprised when the angels brought in her sister, she didn't even know that she was angry at her. When I asked Connie to ask her angels why she was angry, she was told it was because she felt that her sister was a burden. So she stuck her sister's feet in a bucket of cement, waited for it to harden, and then Connie and the angels threw her sister off of a bridge! Connie at this point was feeling strangely empty without the anger she had held onto for so long, so I asked the angels to bring in the colors of cobalt blue and pink, unconditional love, forgiveness of herself and others, and an allowing of herself and others to find their own way home. If in doing this exercise the healee is either not ready to destroy the illusion or feels a need to embrace and love the individual who is brought into their inner vision, I do not interfere and make their process fit my preconception.

Oftentimes the healee will see themselves in their mind's eye as the last person to be 'undone' or 'done in'. What they are dying to are the old perceptions, attitudes and fears that no longer serve them. This process is akin to what is called the death of the shaman, whereby the shaman in deep meditation sees him/herself being eaten by the thing they fear the most. <u>What is being eaten is their fear</u>. When they come out of trance, they are no longer afraid.

Sometimes the healee will bring in God. Many of us are mad at God because we blame Him/Her for the chaos in our lives rather than looking within ourselves. These people are not doing an unholy act! They are blasting apart their own limited misperceptions of God so that the Truth can shine in.

46

In addition there are touch points on the human body which were programmed by the priest Melchizedek that aid in the healing process. (In self-healing I hold crystals in the palms of my hands.) It is not mandatory that a healer use these touch points. It is helpful to utilize these points when the area of involvement on the body of the healee would not be appropriate or too painful for the healer to touch. The healing energy goes right through fabric, so there is no need for the healee to undress; only to wear comfortable clothing. Typically, but not always I start by placing my left hand on the heart chakra and my right hand over the crown. In this way I can check to see that the crown chakra is open. By asking my client to **direct the Light** to different parts of his/her body s/he is getting the idea from the start that they are intricately involved in their own healing process. If a discomfort comes up during the session I can ask them to breath Light energy into the pain. This also gives my client a technique that they can do on their own. An individual working on their own will find it uncomfortable to keep their right hand above their head, but in silent meditation they can visualize Light coming into the crown and then see or feel it going to different parts of the body where healing is needed.

The second thing that I typically do is to clear the mental body and the **mind**. I place the palms of my hands on the head of the humerus, which is the top of the upper arm bone as it drops from the shoulder. My fingertips are pointing down towards their hands. I ask my client not to touch his/her body with their hands. I allow the energy to work for awhile. Then I give suggestions; such as, "Release any judgements that you are still holding on yourself or others." "Release any thoughts of lack and limitation. We live in an abundant universe and are the beloved children of a Father-Mother God who loves us dearly." "Release any old programs that you are still playing about yourself." At sometime during the process I will check to make sure that the energy being released is flowing down their arms by asking if their arms feel heavy. If so I will work my hands down their arms or through the aura. If they say no and I suspect otherwise, I will work my hands down one arm and then ask them if there is a difference between the two arms. If the other arm is heavier, then I will work my hands down that one as well. After the old thought forms are released I say, "Affirm positive attributes that your friends like about you."

To further aid in **mental** healing and to balance and integrate the two hemispheres of the brain, I place my left hand on the forehead and my right hand directly opposite it at the back of the head. If there is a throbbing, I wait until the throbbing stops and then take hold of the misqualified thought forms and lift my hand and arm slowly up through the seven layers associated with each of the major chakras and release it to the Light for transformation, or throw it down to the central fire or to a visualized violet flame (some healers throw 'negativity' into a dish of cold salt water which they place on the floor next to the healee). I have found that it is very helpful to make a counterclockwise circle with my hand first before grabbing the energy and taking it to the Light. In the laying on of hands, if my hands start to feel heavy, this is another indication that something is ready to be released. And again I can either take it up to the Light, or by my intention throw it downwards to the central fire for transformation.

Another method for pulling off negative thought forms is to place my hands on the healee so that they are parallel to the earth. Visualizing or feeling myself becoming an electromagnet, I keep my arms straight. I see the blockages moving up, like lead pellets being drawn up into the arms of a magnet. I lift my arms slowly. When I reach the seventh layer, I flip my hands, which reverses the polarity of your magnet, and sends the psychic debris into the Light for transformation. I can also give the blockages an added push off. No matter if I pull, scoop or lift off misqualified energy, I want to make certain that my own hands are clear before I touch my client again. To do this I wash my etheric arms and hands in a downward movement, or shake my hands and click my fingers over a visualized violet flame. If my hands at any point feel uncomfortably heavy after clearing, I will excuse myself and wash them up to the elbows in cold water. I have never had a client yet who objected to this. The healee wants to release their 'stuff' and they are in a better position to will the misqualified energy into my hands when they know that I am not contracting their disease. Washing hands and arms in cold water up to the elbows is also a very good thing for healers to do after each healing session. Some healers like to say, "disconnect" 3 times after the session to separate themselves from their client. I personally have found that this is unnecessary with Reiki energy.

To **drain misqualified energy** from an area, I place my left hand above the area in the aura and my right hand points downwards towards the central fire within Mother Earth. There is actually a pulling sensation in the left hand. As the misqualified energy is transferred from my left to right hand, I find it is best to keep right arm and hand in front of my body and out of the way of the flying debris. This is also an effective self-healing technique that can be used by anyone. After pulling off misqualified energy and cleansing my hands, I fill the area with Light by placing my hands back on the body, so that the void does not draw in the same or similar 'negative' thought forms. At anytime during the process, my client can help through the use of his/her own visualizations. When I focus my attention and visualize on what is happening in my client, I aid the healing process. These techniques of pulling off and draining misqualified thought forms can be utilized at any of the touch points or anywhere on the body.

After the mental body, I focus my attention on the emotional body and the **emotions**. To do this, I place my left hand on the solar plexus (it is the seat of both repressed anger and joy) and I

48

hold my client's left hand in my right hand. I keep my left hand on the solar plexus no matter what happens. One time a voice came out of one of my clients and told me that it lived just below where my left hand was. I smiled and answered, "That's nice." and I kept my hand on my client's solar plexus. My agreement with Mother-Father God from my first Reiki class has been that S/He knows how much healing energy can be channeled through me and what my spirit guides and angels are able to do. If something comes up, it is because they will be able to handle it. I have also literally had my client's solar plexus expand and push my hand out six inches and more by a thought form at my client's solar plexus. The sensation is like something is trying to punch my hand off from inside my client's body. I keep my left hand where it is no matter what. If I need to pull off, I use my right hand only. I can encourage my client to allow the emotions to come up, feel them and then release them into the ring of fire in the palms of my hands. It is oftentimes uncomfortable for the healee to feel these heavy emotions as they come up, but the constraint that they cause in our physical bodies and our lives is far worse.

One time a man who had been raped grabbed my left hand and threw it off of his solar plexus. He then ran off into another room crying from the emotional pain that had been brought up. What he experienced in those 2 hours of crying and the horror he chose to keep with him, to my mind was far worse than if he had gone on with the healing process for 5 or 10 more minutes. This is not a judgement, he was apparently not ready to release the issue. Like each of us, he could only do what he was capable of in the moment. For those people who are ready to release, I am there to encourage them to let go. There are also people who enjoy wallowing in misery; it is easier to feel depressed than to make the effort and be joyful. While it may be unpleasant to feel misqualified emotional energy patterns, the good news is that when the core of these emotions are felt, transformed and released during a healing session, that's it! They are gone! In order to do this we have to be willing to look within. For example, people who want to control others live outside of themselves; thus, avoiding working on their own issues. The paradox is that in seeking to control others, these people are always giving away their own power. They keep a thumb on one individual or group or issue, and another thumb on something else. Then they are out of thumbs, then they are out of fingers and using their toes until they have given themselves and their power away. True power comes from respect, not fear.

I then move my right hand to their right shoulder. Around the neck is where we keep much of our fear. This fear is visually represented on the astral plane as iron collars, ropes, swords, guillotines, etc. I tell my client what it is that I see, and usually they have already seen it first in their own inner vision. I work to cut, untie, or pull out the implement of shame or death. Necks for many people are a sensitive area, and the release process can be dramatic.

49

Next I will hold their right hand in my right hand. Sometimes I can pull off heavy emotions from the hand itself. Then I move my right hand to their left shoulder. Here I check to see if either anything is still going on in the neck, or if something else is about to begin. In about 20 minutes I have made an "X" over their body with my right hand. Then I will use both of my hands to pull the heavy emotional debris out of the solar plexus, scoop out and then drain the puss-like substance, cauterize the area with cobalt blue color, and have the angels fill the area with Light, colors, tones, herbs, flower remedies and healing symbols. Often times the healee will either smell or see the herbs or flower essences. I have found that the angels and my spirit helpers usually use cobalt blue for cauterizing. It is not only a color of healing and sanitizing, but it also cools down the irritated tissues of the etheric body. In cases where there is diseased tissue, blue seals off the area so that the infection will not spread. Blue is also the only color that I have seen the angels use on cancer; red, orange and even yellow are too hot; green is a color of growth and violet is a color of expansion. For additional information on cancer, I found Hanna Kroeger's , Cancer Begins in the Colon, to be an excellent book (there are several ways to get encrusted fecal matter off of the walls of the intestine). After the solar plexus I then go back to the neck. While I work in the aura, I watch the spirit healers heal the raw etheric tissues around the neck.

After the mental and emotional clearings, I focus on specific areas of the body that need attention using specific touch points for different areas. When I taught these touch points in my Reiki one classes, I would tell people that they are like the ones Jesus used. Every clairaudient would respond by saying, "I am hearing that these are not like the touch points Jesus used, these are the touch points Jesus used." I invite you to meditate on the possibility and try them out for yourself.

For the **bones**, there is an opening between the seventh cervical and the first thoracic vertebrae. These two vertebrae form a boney protuberance at the back of the neck. I place the palm of my right hand over this spot. I take the palm of my left hand and hold it inside the upper left arm. *(The back of the neck will be sore if there is a fracture or break in a bone.)*

For the **spine** I leave my right hand on the back of the neck and place my left hand over the tail bone and let the energy run between my hands. John Sarno, M.D., author of Healing Back Pain, professor of Clinical Rehabilitation Medicine at New York School of Medicine, and attending physician at the Howard A. Rusk Institute of Rehabilitation Medicine at New York University Medical Center, says that pain is a symptom which results from repressed emotions, specifically anger and rage. This is why I do the mental and emotional clearing first unless my

50

client is in such extreme pain that they cannot get past it to identify their issues. In these cases I work on the affected area first and then go back and do the emotional and mental clearing.

For the **tendons & ligaments** the touch points are on the upper right arm. My left hand is over the point where the biceps becomes tendinous. My right hand is over the point where the triceps become tendinous. *(Myrrh oil absorbs into the skin and tendons.)* For **cartilage**, I use these same touch points, and by my intention, I ask that the healing energy be directed there.

The next six touch points are the same use by Hanna Kroeger, a forerunner in the field of homeopathic and herbal medicine. The touch point for the **muscles** is the point just below the flexed calf muscles on the backs of both legs. It is the point where, to be precise, the gastrocenemus becomes tendinous. In the majority of cases it helps if I have my right hand on my client's left side and visa versa. However, a different energy pattern is set up when my hand is on the same side of their body, and either one or both positions may be appropriate to use. If you are so guided, see for yourself which works best. The nice thing about working with elemental energy from Source is that nothing we do is wrong; it is just that some things we do will be more effective. What works with one individual may or may not work with another, which is why it is important for the healer to listen to their angels and holy spirit guides.

For the **ovaries** I place my palms inside the lower leg just below the knees. I do not do this if the woman is pregnant because a miscarriage can result. My students and I have found that these touch points will also work on the male reproductive system as well.

The points for the **central nervous system** are located just below the knees on the front of the leg. For the **kidneys** on the back I place my right over the left kidney and my left hand over the right kidney. For the **ears** I hold the left occipital lobe in my left hand and the palm of their left hand in my right hand. Then I work on the other side. For the **lymph system** I place my right hand under the left armpit and my left hand at the back of the neck.

One time a woman came to me for healing. Her sister had cancer of the breast, it ran in their family. While Sandra and I worked together her sister lay dying in the hospital, not from cancer, but from the damage her heart had received from the radiation. This is actually common, the statistics show that more people die from chemotherapy each year than die of cancer. Now Sandra's breasts had begun to become hard and swollen and the doctor wanted to start running tests and then appropriate therapy on her. Sandra wanted no part of it, which is why she had called me. After the healing session she felt better. Then she was guided to begin a fast she had read about. For 3 to 4 days, every 3 to 4 hours Sandra ate 3 to 4 fresh oranges. The oranges were the only things she ate. She even set her alarm so that she could wake up at night to do this. Sandra told me later that the people she worked with laughed at her, but she didn't care, she did it anyway. Then Sandra went to a natural clinic and bought a homeopathic remedy for the lymph glands. Sandra told me that when she went to the toilet it looked like brown beer foam was coming out of her. But her breasts went back to normal and the healing held. I have heard of other people eating red garlic and red salad onions (they look purple to me), others have taken red clover and chaparral. Linus Pauling advocated Vitamin C. Some people eat a pint of cottage cheese after mixing either a generous spoonful of flax oil or apricot oil in it (cold pressed oil). Other people eat 3 unbleached almonds a day to prevent cancer.

For the **eyes** there are three points: Behind the ear there is a slight indentation in the parietal bone, the angle of the jaw, and at the temporal bone to the side of the eyes. The eyes are an extension of the brain, so the mental and nerve points may also be appropriate. In Mahikari healing for 10 minutes the healer's left hand is raised above their heads to draw in Light, the right hand in the aura radiates Light to the 3rd eye, which is closely associated with the physical eyes. I have found that the touch point for the **skin**, the hollow in the temple bone to the sides of the eyes, can also work on the lens of the eye. An additional point for the **skin**, which brings in collagen and elastin, is to place the palm of the left hand over the 3rd eye.

For the **teeth** we can use the bone point or the nerve points, depending upon where the problem is. For the **gums** I can place my hands over the ears so that the palm of my hand is over the auditory canal. This position will affect the third eye, physical eyes and thymus as well. It is a point that helps connect the third eye and the heart.

For the **lungs**, I place my right hand on the forehead and my left hand opposite the right at the back of the head. An additional touch point is about and inch and a half to either side of the sternum at about the 2nd or 3rd rib. This second touch point is comforting and is also for **weight loss**.

For the **heart**, with my right hand I hold the heel of my client's left hand (the rounded bump above the thumb). I place my left hand on their right shoulder, which opens the heart chakra and works on the right ventricles of the heart. When spirit is through, I place my left hand on their left shoulder. This restores the electrical balance (lemon in water can also do this) and works on the left ventricles of the heart.

In working with diseases, I work with my client's symptoms. For example, in working with multiple sclerosis there is typically a heaviness in the heart and a cloudiness in the brain. So before I work on the points for the nerves, I work with the heart and brain points, and utilize healing techniques for removing the blockages in these two areas. Repeating positive affirmations helps to create well being: "<u>From the Lord God of my being to the Lord God of the Universe</u> *(for example, "I give myself permission to see the whole truth clearly.")* <u>so be it and so it is</u>." Every aspect of our being accepts statements repeated in this manner.

For all **glands**, I place the palms of my hands over the floating ribs. As with the mental clearing, most of the misqualified energy moves down the arms, but out the fingertips only. Beneficial energy comes in through the thumbs. Sometimes my clients can smell the herbs or flower remedies that the angels bring them.

For the **breasts**: My client is sitting or standing and I am facing her right side. <u>First</u> I place the fingertips of my right hand just to the right of her sternum at about the 6th or 7th rib so that I am touching the edge of the sternum. I place the fingertips of my left hand opposite my right hand on the back just to the right of the spine at about the 6th or 7th thoracic vertebrae. Then I push gently and hold. For the <u>second</u> position I leave my left hand on the back and move my right hand under my client's right armpit. I push with my left hand and hold the position. The <u>third</u> position is identical to the first; I move my right hand to the front of the body, push gently and hold. For the <u>fourth</u> position I move my left hand under my client's right armpit, push with my right hand and hold. Again the <u>fifth</u> position is the same as the first and third; I move my left hand to the back, push gently and hold. I then repeat the entire process on the other side. I am facing my client's left side. <u>First</u> I place the fingertips of my left hand just to the left of her sternum at about the 6th or 7th rib. I place the fingertips of my right hand opposite my left hand on the back just to the left of the spine at about the 6th or 7th thoracic vertebrae. Then I push gently and hold. For the <u>second</u> position I leave my right hand on the back and move my left hand under my client's left armpit. I push with my right hand and hold the position. The <u>third</u> position is identical to the first. For the <u>fourth</u> position I move my right hand under my client's left armpit, push with my left hand and hold. The <u>fifth</u> position is the same as the third and first. If necessary I repeat either the entire process, or I will repeat it on only one side of the body, depending upon what is happening with my client. I have seen cysts and tumors diminish or disappear completely within the short period of time it takes to do this. The Sophi-El energy brings up mothering issues or lack thereof, as well as any of my client's own personal feelings of inadequacy as a mother. For **cysts** anywhere, the touch point is the inside ankle of the right foot.

For **Alzheimer's**, there are three points: At the shoulders where the 'V' is formed, at the 2nd or 3rd rib (like the lung point), and above the floating ribs (like the gland point). The difficulty with Alzheimer's is that these people do not like their lives. To escape reality, they check out, they forget. For healings to be successful, individuals often need to make changes in their lives, release those people or aspects that no longer serve the healee's highest and best good, and find the possibilities for creating a new life. Not everyone is willing or able to do this.

As a form of magnetic healing, this process will **lift dropped organs**: A cup or depression is formed at the throat by the heads of the collar bones and the sternum. My client lies on their back. If I am starting at the right side, I gently put the tip of my middle finger of my left hand in the cup and pull slightly towards me. With my right hand I sweep slowly up the right side about six inches above the body and over the top of the head. When I bring my hand back in order to sweep again, I do not want to follow the same path. Either I will keep my hand low, or I will bring it back with my arm fully extended upwards. The sweeping action should be done three times or in multiples of three. I check with my client during the process to find out what s/he is experiencing so that I know when to stop. Then I move my middle finger to the top of the sternum and push down slightly and I repeat this entire process, sweeping up the center as many times as I swept up the right side. In electromagnetic healing, once you touch the body, your hands should remain on the body. So I walk around to the left side keeping contact with my client the whole time. I then gently put the tip of my middle finger of my right hand in the cup, pull slightly towards me, and repeat the sweeping process. Then I move down to the feet and place my hands on the inside of the legs just above the ankles and hold for a few minutes to ground the energy. Personally, I do not recommend that people do magnetic healing unless they are channeling healing energy. Too many times I have seen people give their own energy to the individual that they are working on. We should never have to give of our own energy or take on anyone else's "stuff" as shamans, east Indian gurus and Chi Kung masters have done in the past.

Another form of magnetic healing is a variation of Rosalyn Bruyere's Chelation therapy. Again this is magnetic healing. Once my hands touch the body, I will always have at least one hand on my client at all times. Preparation for magnetic healing involves rubbing the hands together and then rubbing each hand down the opposite arm. Center yourself at your Hara, which is about 2 inches below your belly button. Feel the vertical line running through your center. Follow that line down to the heart of Mother Earth. Ground and feel cobalt blue healing energies from Mother Earth coming back to you. *(Contacting the healing from Mother Earth can be a powerful experience in itself; there have been instances where people have laid down on the earth, slipped into an altered state of consciousness, felt the heart beat of Mother Earth, and were healed.)* Next feel your will center in your solar plexus and follow the vertical line up to the Universal Source, bring back the yellow energy of the sun into the crown and down through the vertical channel. Feel the energies of Mother-Father God meeting in your heart. Visualize clear colors running through all of your chakras. <u>You can also place your hands parallel to the earth and draw in cobalt blue</u>. There are additional rays of color that one can be born with, gathered during a life's journey or initiated into that can be called upon to aid in the healing process.

This particular magnetic technique clears the **joints** as well as the **major chakras**. I start by holding onto the bottom of both feet. I move to the right side of their body, keeping a hold of the bottom of the left foot with my right hand, and I move my left hand to the client's left ankle. I will healing energy to bounce between my two hands. I let my etheric left hand drop into the ankle and use my inner vision, and my sense of feeling. My inner knowing gives meaning to what I am seeing, hearing or feeling. If I find misqualified energy, it may explode in my hand; if not, I grab a hold of it with my etheric hand. I then will my etheric hand into my physical hand and pull up slowly through the seven layers, turn the blockage over to the Light and let the Light transmute it. I may find that this dark spot is like a plug and that often there is mucus behind this blockage. If so, I scoop the mucus out, drain it, cauterize the void with cobalt blue color, fill the area with other colors and healing vibration, and seal it with gold. If, however, the plug has a cord attached to it, I have a time line. I keep pulling out the cord and plugs attached to the cord until I reach the root cause or the last plug. The plugs themselves can represent different occurrences or past lives or both. All the while I am working with my left hand, my right hand remains on the sole of the left foot. While I said earlier that negative energy needs to be pulled off slowly, sometimes this last plug needs to be jerked out. I then scoop out the mucus-like substance and drain the ankle. When it is cleared out, I cauterize the ankle with cobalt blue. Oftentimes I find that the angels bring in herbs, flower remedies, healing tones and symbols. The entire process of pulling out plugs and cords, clearing and filling can also be done at any joint, any touch point, any chakra or on any place on the body that warrants this kind of healing.

I then move my right hand to the sole of the right foot, and my left hand to the right ankle and repeat the above process. For the lower leg: I move my right hand to the left ankle, my left hand to the left knee. Then I move my right hand to the right ankle, my left hand to the right knee. For the upper leg: I move my right hand to the left knee, my left hand to the left hip at the hip joint or the trochanter of the femur. For the right leg I move my right hand to the right knee, and my left hand to the right hip. I then keep my left hand on the right hip joint and move my right hand to the left hip, and I will the energy back and forth between my hands.

Next I move my left hand to the second or creative chakra, and with my right hand I work in the aura above the root chakra. In like manner I move my right hand to the second chakra and my left hand to the navel. I pause and then begin working either in the aura above the second chakra, or with my hand on the second chakra I can will my etheric hand into the body. Next my right hand moves to the navel, my left hand to the solar plexus where I work on the solar plexus. Then my right hand moves to the solar plexus, my left hand to the heart. And so it goes as I move up the chakras; my right hand to the heart, my left hand to the throat. My left hand to the third eye, my right hand to the throat. My left hand to the crown or the top of the head, my right hand to the third eye. To complete the process I work up each arm; palm to wrist, wrist to elbow and elbow to shoulder joint. I can also ask the healee to turn over and then work on the back chakras or vertebrae.

This same process can be done from the healee's left side using the left hand to do the work while the right hand sends energy into the body. Or I can alternate working and sending with each hand. It may also be appropriate to work on only one or a few areas of the body. For example, this technique can be used on individual vertebrae with healees with spinal problems, or on the points of the fingers.

There is a Universal palette or rainbow of colors that is available to everyone. To reach the Universal colors, I focus at the crown and then move up the vertical energy line, past the soul star chakra (located about 6 inches above the crown), and past the soul. Spirit guides and the angels will help me to find the rainbow. The right colors come back through the vertical energy line and out my hands. The more healing energy the healer is channeling, the stronger the colors will be. Strength does not necessarily mean the depth of the color, for sometimes pastel colors are what is needed.

To **clear the chakras** I start at the crown and work down the front and then up the back. I spread my fingers and make claws out of my hands; the Reiki energy acts like a magnet in the palm and draws out misqualified energy. I move my hands slowly through the chakra in the aura from left to right three times and then right to left three times. I throw the misqualified energy into a violet fire that I have psychically created, or into a dish of cold salt water, or by my intention down to the central fire for transformation. I have found that people with low or no energy benefit greatly from having the root chakra cleared; one woman told me she felt like she had suddenly woken up. We also have chakras at the navel and the small of the back, which is referred to as the door of life or the meng ming. To **clear the aura** I start above the top of the head, again make claws out of my hands and rake down down the center and on both sides through the aura both front and back. I repeat each movement three times.

To **close the session** I place my left hand on the solar plexus. My right hand on the left groin, the line that is made between your torso and your leg when you sit down (there is a long tendon there). Then I switch hands, placing my right hand on the solar plexus and my left hand on the right groin. This is also a touch point for **childhood issues**.

Obviously, I would not have time to use all of the above techniques in one session. It would be an exhausting healing marathon for everyone involved. I work with my client's symptoms and do what is appropriate in the moment and what I am guided to do. Sessions can last anywhere from a half hour to an hour and a half, and oftentimes it is necessary for the healee to have 3 sessions. Sometimes my client leaves his/her body and is unconscious during some or most of the time. When the healee is present in his/her body, I like to keep checking in to find out what's happening, and also to have them visualize and work with the process. Sometimes people will call just prior to a session and cancel because they are not feeling well. I tell them that it maybe happening because something is coming up to be healed, and if they look within and ask, this might be a very good time to come in for a session. Either way it's up to them to decide.

Frequently, I work with crystals. The ascended masters, Aliazor and Luciar, work with all crystals. Everything including crystals has a consciousness and comes from Mother-Father God, and different crystals have various properties that can be used in healing. For example, black stones such as obsidian or red rubies can be used for grounding by placing them next to the feet. As red garnet is a stone for the blood and the touch point for **blood** is over the heart chakra (sternum and thymus), I could place a garnet at the heart chakra. This is also the trigger point for **arteries** and **veins**.

Laser crystals and the pointed end of any crystal can be utilized effectively by the healer in the aura. Blockages in the aura, in the chakras and in the body can be cut out using the laser crystal or point of a crystal in the aura over the affected area. The client's skin is never scratched, never cut; this type of psychic surgery is nonevasive. Diane, of the New Spirit Crystal Gallery in Milwaukee, was told by her guides that in using the point of a crystal for healing that it is important to convey to the crystal what exactly it is that you want the crystal to do. Clockwise circles can be made with the crystal as you move in closer to the body either over the diseased area or over a chakra. The point of the crystal, which is the most powerful part, can be used to pull off misqualified energy, and again the healer makes known to the crystal what the intention is. Very specifically, the point of a crystal sends out energy, the healer in this case needs to ask the crystal to act as a magnet. In using the point to pull off 'negative' energy, the healer can pull straight out on a beam of visualized light, or use counterclockwise circles. The blockages can then be taken to the Light for transformation or sent down to the central core of fire. Diane pulls these energies out of the healee's entire aura before sending it off for transformation. The healee can acknowledge, bless, and talk to the blockages as they come up. Sometimes it is important to ask these blockages, "What is it I am to learn from you?" The answer can come as a visual, a feeling, auditory message or as an inner knowing.

The base of a crystal can be placed on the body over the diseased area or chakra with the point facing up. In this way misqualified energy is pulled up and out. Before placing the crystal on the body, it is helpful for the healer to use the pointed end of a crystal in the aura to break up or start moving misqualified energy. Draining the puss-like substance behind the blocks can be done by holding the left hand palm down in the aura over the affected area; the right hand holds the crystal and is pointing it down towards the central core of fire. Sean Grealy holds a pendulum in his right hand. The crystal moves in counterclockwise circles as the misqualified energy is being released. The circles become smaller and smaller, and when the pendulum stops, the draining is completed. The void can be filled with Light by placing crystals on the body (Katrina Raphael has some excellent books out on this, or the healer can work intuitively in the placement of crystals). Healers can work in the aura with crystals, or tune into the crystals, and in this manner the healer enhances the energy and work that the crystals are doing. Healing energy can be drawn in by raising the left arm (elbows and wrist unbent) towards the Light, and placing the right hand in the field above the void or directly on the area.

When I am through (or sometimes during the healing) I clear the stones in cold water, in sunshine or I place them on a clear quartz cluster. Smudging with sage and cedar (sage clears, and because the Universe does not like voids, cedar brings in beneficial energies) also works with crystals. While some healers use rubbing alcohol instead of cold water for clearing their arms and hands, I personally have found that crystals do not respond well to rubbing alcohol.

Crystal shops such as The New Spirit Crystal Gallery, where the owners understand and appreciate the esoteric value of crystals, can provide assistance in purchasing crystals. Although I have also found crystals that call out to me. Once I hesitated before purchasing a $500 healing stone and I asked, "Are you sure you want me to buy this?" My guide, Straight Arrow, replied, "Why do you think we are getting you the money?"

There is a wide variety of ways in which people release what we call negative energies. Some people shake (shivering timbers at their very foundation) and/or cry like Deborah Fiorill did on an angel segment that was shown on Connie Chung's CBS program "Eye to Eye". Other people get very cold and need to be covered by blankets. Some people sweat. Some people have to talk out their problems. My job as a healer is to stay out of judgement and love people where they are. Also, everything that comes up in a session is absolutely confidential! The people whose stories I have included in this book gave me permission to do so. They felt that their experiences might be of benefit to others. Where I felt examples were relevant, I used a different name.

Two of the most important things that all healers, including myself, have to remember are: One, to feel sorry for someone else comes from our own mental distortions and is a judgement; compassion comes from the heart. Secondly, a person has to ask for a healing, otherwise it just isn't going to happen or the healing will not hold. Once I invited a friend of Charlotte's and mine up to her Manhattan apartment. In the 4 hours that Charlotte and I worked on him using all of the tools that we knew, he possibly moved a millimeter if that. He wasn't interested in healing his issues! How arrogant of me to think that I could play God! As healers, healing energy flows through us. We may be able to learn to bilocate and even multilocate, but we are not omnipotent. Only God is omnipresent!

I used to wait on tables. At the time it was the only job I could get that would allow me to support my 2 children and put myself through college. Once the wife of one of my high school classmates came in and was telling me how she and her husband were getting a divorce. Then out of the blue she asked me if she should have him call me. My first impression was to say , no. As she went on talking I stopped to think, I had just had a vivid prophetic dream concerning this man. This was quite a coincidence, so I told her to have him call. He never did. He wasn't interested in knowing! How presumptuous of me to think I could step in and save their marriage! So through my own experiences I have learned to stay out of other people's business, which includes my own family. Unless they ask me for help or advice I stay out of the picture. I also have no desire to waste my time, or the time of my spirit guides and angels.

Other people serve as mirrors, reflecting back to us our own innate qualities. But every coin has its flip side. When we admire people who hold such attributes as beauty, integrity, and wisdom; and abilities such as those of a fine pianist or sculpture, we are also seeing ourselves. We can only see who we are. There is much good, much potential lying within each and everyone of us. But it remains an embryo until we recognize and nourish it.

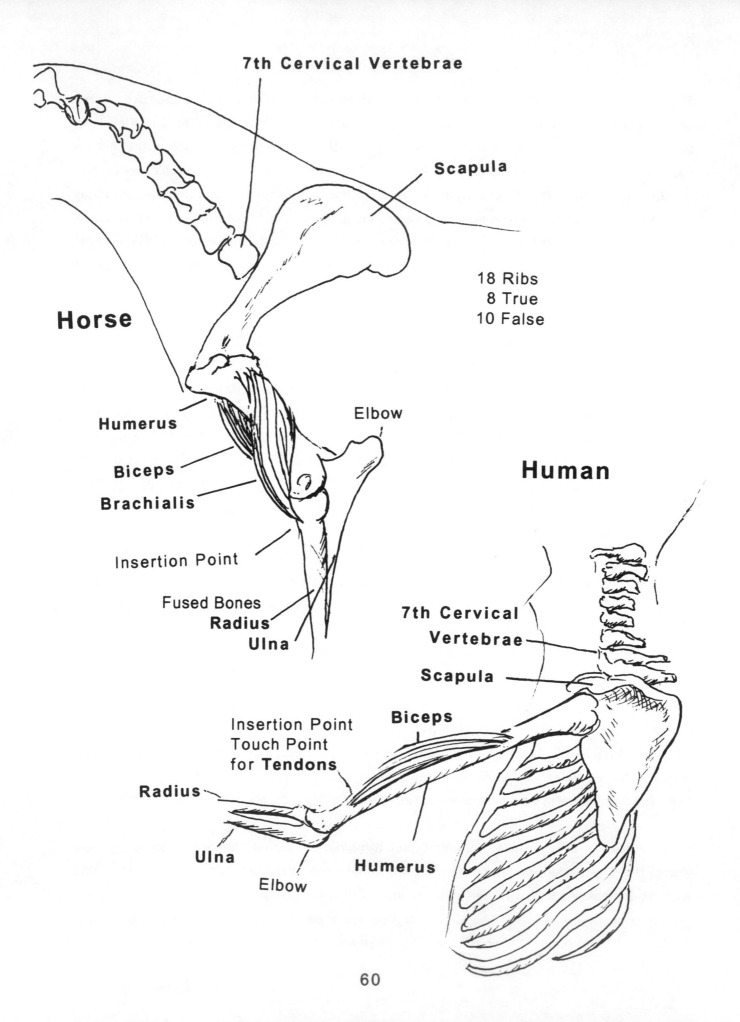

7th Cervical Vertebrae

Scapula

Horse

18 Ribs
8 True
10 False

Humerus

Elbow

Biceps

Brachialis

Human

Insertion Point

Fused Bones
Radius
Ulna

7th Cervical
Vertebrae

Scapula

Insertion Point
Touch Point
for **Tendons**

Biceps

Radius

Ulna

Elbow

Humerus

60

Animals and Healing

If it is true that animals once had an oversoul, because of their service, sacrifice and love for humanity, they have developed their own individual souls. Ask any pet owner. They will tell you not only about the unique personality of their companion, but also of the quality we call unconditional love that they receive on a daily basis from their pet. It is why an animal's absence is experienced profoundly with their passing. Unconditional love is an attribute that only a spirit filled with God can give. This is a soul!

Each animal group brings to earth qualities which native Americans refer to as animal medicine. These abilities are well described in story form in the book, Medicine Cards by Sams & Carson. There is joy of hummingbird, femininity of otter and power of horse. Even the 6-legged mosquito serves a purpose. Tonya Butts watched a mosquito land on her leg, and rather than smashing it, she communicated with it and asked, "I'm sure you have something to say, what is it?" The mosquito answered, "I suck out fear in small amounts at a time so that you won't be overwhelmed. I bring fear to the surface so that you can scratch beyond it." That particular bite left no welt. When humanity moves beyond its fear there will be no more need for mosquitoes.

Many spiritual traditions throughout the world used an animal's hide or bird's feathers to connect to the animal's power. In our age it is not spiritually correct to intentionally kill a member of a species on the brink of extinction; thus, there is no benefit gained from these hides, feathers, etc.. In fact, the opposite is true! The higher, stronger, conscious communication and expression of animal medicine is accomplished by utilizing the vibrational pattern alone. Working to save wilderness and wildlife connects us to the animal's energy patterns. Drawing in animal qualities can be done in journey work, meditation, or by using a painting or photograph that reflects the spirit and medicine of the creature. Artwork that is highly detailed does not necessarily contain energy; artwork that has energy may not necessarily have the kind of vibration we want around our homes and places of work. It is like purchasing crystals, they pick us. Even pets pick their owners; watch a litter of puppies or kittens sometime and observe how individuals will perform when the right person comes along. When we don't buy the things we love, be they paintings, crystals or pets, we are always sorry later.

Animals go through reincarnation cycles just like we do. It is the reason why some individuals are wiser and more conscious that others. For the most part a soul stays within a particular species. This is; however, not always the case. Often when there is an exception to the rule, the animal's actions will be out of context with his/her species. Ziggy, a wondrous, fun-loving cat, has never been a cat before. He was totally dependant upon Janis, his sister, to teach him how to be one. Among other things, he had to learn to be graceful. My daughter, Jennifer, and I have watched him walk across the back of the sofa and suddenly, for no reason, fall off. Not slip, but flip off. He often acted like a horse that had been brought into the house from the barn. Psychically, the presence that precedes him is one of a much larger animal.

People who are extremely cruel to animals, as part of their soul's lesson, may reincarnate as an animal to walk in another's hoofs or paws so as to experience the animal's point of view. The nature of this living Truth and reality is what we call karma, and through it we understand another's life experience; we learn tolerance and perfect love. Karma is more frequently realized within a species. That is, we go back and forth; in one lifetime the slave trader, the next the slave; in one lifetime the Israelite, the next the Palestinian; in one lifetime the Hindu, the next the Moslem. And so it goes round and round in a circle until we learn to see perfection and God in everything; that we are all One.

If we so wish, we can ask to be reincarnated as a particular animal. If we love a species dearly, it is a way to open the heart to unconditional love. I heard a story told that Christ once incarnated as a white horse, and anyone who saw this horse never forgot him. I do not know if it is true or not, but it is certainly possible. The difference between having to and wanting to reincarnate as a four legged or winged can be dramatic.

My Great Aunt Hatti, who died in her 90's, said everyday of her life, as long as anyone can remember, that she was going to come back as an eagle. My Aunt June once told her, "Are you crazy, you'll be eating rats and snakes." Aunt Hatti retorted, "I won't care." She's right! I bet that she is soaring high above on eagle's wings at this moment. When she catches her prey she is most likely overjoyed. What we focus on we create. We are drawn to what we love as well as to what we hate. It is part of a grand Universal plan, which looks more like a joke when we begin to take ourselves too seriously.

I was watching the "Arsenio Hall Show" with my son one evening. The comedian was holding up a picture of a man, and laughing so hard that he could hardly speak. What would you like to be when you grow up? Doctor? Lawyer? Teacher? How about horse? That's what the man in the picture wanted to be, only he wanted to be horse now! He went so far as to live in a stall in the barn and pulled a pony cart. Yes, I would bet that this man is now reincarnated as a horse, of course. What we ask for we get! Especially those requests petitioned on our last earth walk day.

Animals communicate with us, we are the ones who are not always listening. Many people have had experiences with animals that is beyond what could be called simple response behavior. One spring day I had my windows open enjoying the fresh air. I heard a robin wildly scolding, so I looked outside. I saw my first cat, Muffin, in a pine tree next to the front door. All I could see was her tail and rear end. She was going after the baby robins. I grabbed Muffin and took her inside, much to her dismay. The adult robin was looking on from a nearby elm, and I knew that she would be returning to her nest. Several days later I heard her calling wildly again. Looking around I saw Muffin sleeping on a chair. Then I looked out my front window and saw the robin sitting in the small cherry tree, which grew next to the pine. She was surrounded by black birds. Black birds love to feast on baby robins. I went outside and chased the black birds away. The robin remained in the cherry tree even while I looked upon her in amazement. To this day I know that robin was calling me to help her. Animal heroism is another example of both compassion as well as higher response patterns.

Animal communicators work psychically with animals to help their owners find the cause of difficulties or disease, and the nature of injuries. A stable called an animal communicator out because they were having problems with a horse that did not want to work. In communicating with him, she found out that in his last lifetime he lived a particularly hard life as a man. The only horses he ever saw were out in a field grazing all day. He envied their life and not fully understanding his request, he asked to be reincarnated as a horse in his next lifetime. If he had more fully understood the reincarnation cycle, he might have asked simply for a lifetime in which he could rest. We really do get whatever we ask for. Someone once told me that God knows two words, ohm and yes! Now reincarnated as horse, this particular soul was resentful because he had to work. He wanted to be out in the sunshine eating grass and playing. The animal communicator had to delicately tell him that if he didn't work, his owners didn't want him and neither would anyone else except the glue factory. She worked with the animal to help him find joy in carrying a rider.

Bear Shaman is an Alaskan Malamute (half wolf/half Husky), who lives at Ishpiming, a new age retreat center constructed over the center of a huge energy vortex in northern Wisconsin. In his previous life Bear Shaman was a Native American shaman on these same lands. Through a man and woman channeling team known as Twin Trees, Bear asked permission to be born and brought to live at Ishpiming, where he would continue working for Mother Earth and her children. While I was working at Ishpiming the summer Bear was still a puppy, I was impressed to initiate Bear as a Reiki Master. Almost a year later Twin Trees again tuned into the soul of the shaman. He talked about the healing work he was doing, "When I dig in the ground with my large paws, I unearth the prayers that have been said for Mother Earth. And when I roll on my back, I spiral them up to Heaven."

Animals think and communicate in pictures. The most successful horse riders and trainers visualize what they want the horse to do before they physically ask the horse to do it. It is like visually playing a movie in your head just ahead of what you expect from the horse. For example, at a specific spot in the arena you want your horse to change gaits and move in a 20 meter circle. Visualize that place, your cue and the gait as you approach your mark. It is like playing a musical instrument and reading a measure ahead of what you are actually playing.

In psychically receiving messages back from the animal, we need to tune in. First step is to open my heart and send love to the animal. This opens both our heart centers; and as the heart is the gate to the upper chakras, it also serves to open the psychic sending and receiving centers. The act of giving love reassures the animal, and bonds us. Sometimes it helps to touch the animal while I am doing the reading. To make sense out of the visual pictures I am seeing, I also need to tune into my inner feelings and knowing. I tell the owner what I am seeing. I speak it even though it doesn't make any sense to me. Once in Santa Fe I tuned into Chantel Quincy's cat and saw an unlikely desert home. I described it anyway and said, "There probably isn't anything like that around here!" Chantel responded, "Oh, yes there is!" And apparently it was a place of some distance away where she didn't want her cat to be. Together the pet's owner and myself make sense out of the visuals and figure out why and where the animal is in discomfort, and what the core issue is.

I bought my horse, Abez, for $500, the price of horse meat, because nobody else wanted him. He had been excessively abused and beaten by a spiritually unconscious man. Abez's behavior was one of a shell-shocked veteran of war. He had been with many different trainers afterwards, but nobody could do anything with him. In large part because I loved Abez and he loved me unconditionally in return, I was able to work slowly with him. Initially I rewarded him for approximate behaviors; actually I was giving him treats for things you would be reprimanding most other horses for. As he muscled back up and became ridable he demonstrated 4 fantastic gaits, speed, power, agility and flexibility. We once jumped 6 feet from a standstill. It was not a planned event. I was riding him towards a small 2 foot jump. For some reason he

64

panicked and stopped just before the rail. I don't know how he was able to do this, maybe it was the quarter horse in him, but he picked up all 4 of his feet and moved to the right. Then he picked up all 4 of his feet and moved to the left. At this point we were directly in front of a 6-foot gray standard. Only my right foot was in a stirrup as he rocked back onto his haunches. At that point I grabbed mane and rein because in the moment it flashed to me that if I tried to stop him, we would both go over. I never realized before that when you jump that high on a horse, as you move up with the horse, there is a point at which you are actually standing upright. I managed to stay on Abez because when he landed, he didn't take off. One dressage trainer I worked with felt that Abez could have been champion of not just the Midwest, but of the United States.

Besides this, Abez was a beautiful chestnut horse; his body was the color of copper, and his mane and tail were flaxen. One vet told me that Abez had the best qualities of all the breeds. He had wide quarter horse hips, tall shoulders like a saddlebred, the racing line of the thoroughbred, and the graceful arching neck and dish pan eyes of the Arab. With all this I can look back with absolutely perfect hindsight and see that rather than boarding Abez, he should have been kept on my own private farm. I was not in prosperity consciousness, however, to be able to do this. When Dolores Arechavala did a reading for me shortly after Abez's death, she told me that I was not to have any regrets, that both Abez and I learned and grew greatly through our experiences.

Two owners of two different riding stables where I boarded Abez rode my horse without permission when I wasn't around. The first women used to take my horse out early in the morning and when she couldn't, she would lease him out to whom I later learned was a medical professional. When I came out to ride Abez I would find him either worn out or injured mysteriously. She or the man she leased him to managed to injure Abez on four different occasions. She offered to buy my "miserable horse" from me and sell me a "decent ride." One day one of her hands became frozen into what looked like a disfigured bird's leg and claw, and it stayed that way. When we inflict needless pain upon an animal, who is basically defenseless, karma comes back more than a hundred fold. I prayed for her, not realizing at the time what she was doing to Abez, and the claw went away. If I had known, I would have moved him first and then prayed for her. What can I say, I'm human. Her karma didn't end with the claw.

One of the lessons we are here to learn is to **pay attention!** Having missed all of the small clues, the Universe threw larger and larger ones into my face. When Abez and I jumped 6 feet, the owner/trainer of the stable was present and she laughed until she realized that I hadn't fallen off, then she stopped. Nobody else was laughing. Another day I was riding Abez in the arena while she was giving a lesson to another rider and every time I rode Abez past her he snorted at her. And finally, one morning I went out to the barn after riding him the night before to have a look around. None of the horses had been turned out, they were still eating their breakfast. When I went into Abez's stall, even though I had cleaned him up the night before, he had mud packed solidly into all four hoofs and twigs and burrs in his tail. That is when I decided to move Abez.

The next barn I moved him to, the owner tried to sell him. I don't know how she was going to tell me that a twelve-hundred-pound horse disappeared? When I discovered her plans, I moved him immediately, not wishing to pursue this particular drama further.

The next stable was uneventful, it was like God giving us a coffee break, as Pari Dulac would say. I kept Abez there for a couple of years. During this period the owners became increasingly busy with outside endeavors to the point that they were hardly ever around. The day I saw an empty 4-horse trailer pull up with nobody on the premises I made arrangements to move Abez.

This particular owner/trainer where I moved Abez to had a good reputation. In particular I learned how to relax on Abez and let him move my seat at all four gaits. With what I had learned from other European and American instructors, Abez and I were really getting the hang of riding. However, I could tell that he didn't particularly like her. One day when I was taking a lesson from her, she walked over to us. Abez reached over and bit her on the arm. He had never done this before or since. I knew then that something was very wrong. I could also see it in her eyes. She had not been hurt, as she was fully padded in a ski sweater and snowmobile suit. The next day when I went out to the stable, my horse was injured and somebody had used my saddle. I knew this because I always uncinched both sides of my girth, not just one, and would then lay it across the top of the saddle. Because of Abez's big shoulders, my saddle had what is called, a large tree. My saddle would not have fit any of the other horses at this barn as they were small Arabs. And the only person who could ride my horse or any boarder's horse and not be caught would be the owner of the riding stable.

Again we moved, this time closer to my home, which was nice for a change. When we arrived Cathy, who had boarded her horse at the first stable I mentioned while Abez was there, came out to greet us. Then she started to go on and on about the fact that there wasn't a resident trainer at this stable. Finally I asked her what she was talking about and she answered, "There won't be anyone to ride your horse everyday the way _____ (the owner/trainer of the first stable I described) used to do for you. I said, "Excuse me?" In that moment I was horrified at how unconscious I had been. At how much I had brushed aside or excused. During that entire time period it seemed like I was always doing healings on my horse. I even initiated him into Reiki and other rays of touch healing in an effort to save his life and help him heal. However, the injuries stopped when I stopped blaming other people for my horse's misfortune and I asked, "What is Abez doing to draw unconscious people, traumatic events, and injuries to himself?"

Abez's stubbornness had helped him to survive horrific abuse and beatings; now it no longer served him. What I needed to do was to help him to transform and release this energy, and to encourage him to use his energy in a positive expression; to make a shift in consciousness and look at things in a different way. That is, willfulness without consideration for my needs is counterproductive; audacity and the persistence of carrying out a task to its greatest conclusion is an attribute. When Abez made this shift, he and I became an even stronger team.

This came about after Abez hit bottom. He reached his particular low point while I was in Los Angeles at the Whole Life Expo, the same expo where I did the healing demonstration on Beverly Henson. He had injured his right eye, and because the owner of the barn had had an accident himself, Abez was left unmedicated and untreated in his stall for the eight days I was in California. When I returned, his right eye was blind and had turned a pale powder blue. There is a time and a place for allopathic medicine. I called the vet. When he arrived I asked him to give Abez penicillin, but he gave me eye cream which I already had. He said that it wasn't necessary to give Abez penicillin, that there was a triple antibiotic in the eye cream. There I was with 2 one-ounce tubes of eye cream and a twelve-hundred pound horse. That night when I returned to the barn to reapply the eye cream, I found that my horse hadn't eaten, the infection in his eye had spread throughout the rest of his body. A friend once told me that to a horse, food is god. For a horse not to eat is extremely serious. I knew that if he didn't get penicillin that evening that he would be down by morning. If a horse lies down because they do not feel good, it's difficult to get them back up. If they are down too long, their insides stop moving. The shot of penicillin I gave him that evening immediately helped his energy level, he started eating, and he began healing. Between the eye cream, penicillin, hands-on and distant healing, Abez was seeing out of a brown eye within two weeks. It is interesting to note that both Beverly and Abez evolved into accomplished healers in their own right.

Abez's injuries typically occurred just prior to making, or my considering making arrangements to show him. Abez was telling me that he did not want to be a show horse. Abez and many other animals, especially those higher on the reincarnation journey, understand what is being spoken. So I explained to him that I was OK and respectful of his wish, that I wanted to be able to enjoy riding him skillfully, and I wanted him to be comfortable, happy, and healthy when I wasn't around. What Dolores Arechavala also told me in her reading was that Abez's subconscious was afraid that someone would steal him from me if I started showing him. When I asked her if his concerns were legitimate, Dolores answered affirmatively. He was a wonder horse. Three people told me within a week after buying him that Abez was a reincarnation of Man 'O War. But to the world his greatness was never revealed. With my promise to him, Dolores told me that his fears were dispelled and he was at peace the last several years I owned him.

I bought Abez when he was 9-years old. I owned him, or he owned me for nine years. When he was 18-years old he decided to make his transition. He had accomplished his goals, learned his lessons, and as a sacrifice for me he went on. He felt that if he moved to the Arizona deserts with me that he would hold me back by demanding too much of my time, keeping me from the work I had to do.

I had called the vet out on a Monday for what I thought was a minor problem. It wasn't! After the vet described the surgery, which he would have to wait a week for, and afterwards endure a painful 4-week recovery period, I decided not to put him through that kind of torture. He had been healed miraculously before; this time he wasn't talking any healing energy. Or what energy he was taking, he was using to control the pain.

Early Tuesday evening I had Abez put down. I spent the afternoon in a field of clover with him saying goodbye. I watched him graze, patted him and fed him an occasional apple. I knew he was suffering and that his condition was going downhill quickly. On Sunday he had rolled in the grass; Tuesday he couldn't even lie down. I told Abez what a joy he had been in my life, and how much both of us had grown in those nine years. I told him about the beautiful place he was going to, and that soon all of his pain would be gone. All of nature came out to say goodbye and to help Abez. At one point I saw a Galactic Confederation ship come down from the clouds saying, we're here to help too. There were times that afternoon when the heavens seemed to open and Abez and the sky and I were one. The vet came at 6:30. My image was the last he saw before he laid down. As he slept, waiting for the anesthesia to reach his heart, I kept encouraging him to go to the Light. I can still hear his last breath. Just as the soul comes into the baby's body with the first breath, the soul leaves with the last breath. Three white swans had been swimming in the large pond in front of the farm when I arrived that day and left unseen shortly after Abez died. They had never been there before or come back since. To this day I believe that they were three angels who manifested to assist him.

68

When I got home that evening, I called my friend, who is an extremely accurate psychic and healer, Katherine Ettmayer, to help me tune into Abez to see if he had made his way to the Light. She felt that he was still at the farm. We both sent distance healing. He still wasn't going. I journeyed there; that is, an aspect of myself went to the farm to assist him. Abez did not go to the Light, Abez went into the Universe and became a star. When a soul through its various incarnations masters its lessons, develops gifts and talents, opens the heart to unconditional love and feels compassion, their transition is like Abez's; oneness with All There Is. It is the same transition that Jesus made; it is one that we all can make.

Within the year before his death, Abez had completed the sacred marriage with his own twin flame, that aspect of his own soul which held his other 2/3's feminine and 1/3 masculine energy. A friend and I watched on another plane as Abez and the white mare played and danced to the rhythms of the spheres. They were having great fun. At one point they pretended to be carousel horses. A silver cord of love runs between their two hearts forever. When Abez died he became what we call a master or an avatar; he became one with the Universe and co-creator with Mother-Father God.

Abez's transition made it possible for other horses to do the same. Jake, who is channeled through a medium named Cocorah, told me that with Abez's transformation and the July 1994 comet hitting Jupiter, which is horses, the energy of horse is raising to equal that of dolphin and whale on this planet. It is like this, the first millionaire in the United States created the way for a hundred more to become millionaires, and they in turn did so likewise. It is also true that in order for any of us to go forward, we must bring at least one other soul up to our level, and we get lots of help from the Universe along the way if we are open. Scarcity, be it money or illumination of the spirit, is an illusion. Jealousy looks at the successful individual and has not the vision to see that a way has been opened for themselves. Opened not to recreate the identical life experience of another, but rather to take the core idea and create something that is unique. In this manner humans and the planet we live on are able to evolve upwards.

Katherine went on to tell me the evening that Abez transcended, that he would be sending me healing energy that evening in a dream. I finally fell asleep that night with tears rolling out of my eyes. My heart felt like it had been cut out of my body, and in my chest was a large gaping hole. In the middle of the night I was awakened. I had been dreaming about Abez, and as I lay in bed powerful waves of love and healing moved through me and continued in that form into the next day.

Death is far harder on those who are left behind then it is for the soul who has decided to journey through the passageway home. Any 3-dimensional plane gives an illusion of separation, when in reality there is none. Because I am in contact with other planes of reality I both know and feel Abez's present joy. When the grieving period was over, I was not left with an enormous, permanent sense of loss, as do people who have been denied the existence of other realities. Abez's physical death; however, did leave a huge hole in my life. When I was home I used to go out to the barn 4 or 5 times a week to see him and ride him. He was my friend. He is still my friend, but now he is also my power animal, a spirit guide and he aids in the healing work that is done through me.

I kept my healing appointments even the week after Abez died so that my mind would not constantly be preoccupied with him. On Friday I was working on a woman with a blockage that she could not release. Suddenly, in my mind's eye I saw Abez's left rear leg come in and kick it out of her. I opened my eyes and looked at my client. Her eyes shot open and she said, "I don't know what you just did, but it was like a cannon ball just left my body." How could I tell her that my horse just kicked her?

I have been told by numerous psychics that the angels take me up to him at night so that I can ride him. I know this is true. Sometimes in the morning I awaken with soreness in the same tendons that had been injured in the car accident and that used to bother me after I rode Abez. Only the pain is getting less and less, and I am getting better and better.

While it would certainly be my personal preference for everyone to be well, alive and happy, I have had to learn that my job is to be a vehicle for healing energy to come through. I have to allow my clients and friends, be they four legged, two legged or winged, to develop and grow at their own pace and love them where they are. I also have to allow them to make their transitions when they are ready. I told the owner of a golden retriever that I worked on that I felt that their dog wanted to go on. Instead of looking within and checking it out, she had her dog's badly infected, left rear leg removed to the top joint. Six months later the dog died of cancer of the lungs. Another six months later I saw the owner again. She said that if she had to do it over again that she would not put her dog through all the pain it had to endure after surgery.

One of the most difficult things for us to do, is to be joyful for someone who has gone to the Light. In our gladness we assist them in that transition. The grieving process is necessary, but to grieve without also rejoicing for our loved ones, for the joy and wonder that is now theirs, is to hold them earth bound.

Modern religions have not only taken God's Majesty away from us, but they also do not prepare us for the dying process or death. I believe one reason some people hold tenaciously onto life, long after the spirit is ready to make its passage, is because they do not want to sit on a white cloud for eternity playing a harp, and if they are lucky, an occasional French horn. After the soul leaves the body, it has 3 days in which to go to the Light. All great mysticisms speak of this. In that 3-day period each one of us has to get through the thought forms and emotions that we created in life. Dark, heavy ones, like control and greed, are harder to get through. If the soul cannot do it in 3 days, it becomes earth bound and confused. Sometimes they do not know that they are even dead; our astral body looks very much like our physical body. This is why it behooves each one of us to work through our issues of fear, hate, envy, etc. now while in body. It is a lot easier!

Most souls, after making the transition, are taken to a place of healing and rest. We review our lives and decide or <u>judge for ourselves</u> what was missed, what we still need to work on, what we learned, etc. When they are ready, people and animals can come back to guide and assist those whom they loved in life. Frequently, psychics in readings will describe a deceased pet who is traveling spiritually with their former owner. Nancy Moore says that there isn't a day that goes by that she doesn't think about Trena. She knows that her dog is an angel and is always with her. Our guides are here to help and assist us. When you see or hear them with your psychic senses, ask three times if they have come in the name of Jesus or if they are in Divine Truth. Even with animal spirits, remember to check. It is of notable consequence that we do so.

Because animals have chakras and souls, if they are ready and willing, they can be initiated into healing energies. After initiating Abez into Reiki, I felt that my cats were asking me to initiate them and I did. Afterwards, whenever anyone would come to my home for a healing, Janis and Ziggy would jump up on the table with my client. Ziggy would usually go to the feet to ground the energy. Ziggy does not under ordinary circumstances lie down at our feet. Janis would always go to the spot where the individual was having a pain or problem, and my clients could feel healing energy coming from her paws. Janis' eyes change when she does healings; you can see that she is in a trance state. I have found consistently that after initiating animals into healing rays that they become more intelligent and more aware on all levels. I encourage my students to consider initiating their pets into Reiki.

All animals have the same bones, muscles and tendons that we as humans have. They are elongated or shortened, combined or slanted. For scientists to call animals' bones, muscles and tendons by different names than what we call the human equivalent thereof, is actually confusing the issue. For example, a horse has more thoracic vertebrae than I do, but my femur bone (upper leg bone) is actually longer than a horse's. What we think of as the top of a horse's back leg is actually his knee. The femur angles upwards and backwards, connecting to the hip at the joint. What we think of as a horse's knee is actually his ankle, and all the bones from that point down are bones of the foot (metatarsal bones). Horses and other hoofed animals literally walk on their toes. Their nail or hoof is much thicker and more developed than our toenails. The same is true for a horse's front legs. What looks like the top of his front leg is actually his elbow. His humerus (upper arm bone) angles upwards and forwards, connecting to the scapula at the joint. The scapula, which is quite large, angles upwards and backwards. The withers is formed by the cartilage extension of the scapula. In a horse the radius and ulna (bones of our lower arm) are fused together. Again what we think of as his knee is actually his wrist and contains the bones of the hands. What we think of as his lower leg is actually fused metacarpal bones; the hock is the sesamoid bone, and below that are the phalanges. He is walking on his fingertips. When a horse rears up, or when we bend over, we are better able to see our similarities. Look at the dinosaur skeletons in the museum; it is not just monkeys who resemble us. Physical bodies are a theme in variation in the eyes of the Creator. There are always reminders that Mother-Father God has provided more than one way to get to heaven.

What this has to do with healing animals is this, the same touch points that I use on my two-legged clients, I can also use on my four-legged clients. I can also use other healing techniques I described in the last chapter and adapt them to the animal I am working on. To bring in the **Light** by placing my hand on a horse's sternum (heart chakra) and over his head would be too long a reach for me and most other people that I know. Besides, horses do not like to be touched on the top or their heads, it makes them very nervous. So before I even begin I want to be aware of the individual animal's character as well as traits particular to his/her species. All the while I am working, I like to have someone the animals knows at the head reassuring him/her. As with my human clients, I work with an animal's current symptoms. With animals it is more difficult because their symptoms usually have been going on longer than the outward physical manifestation that their owner noticed. This is one reason why a veterinarian's job is difficult. I feel animal communication or inner communication is necessary for both owners and healers. One horse's spine and back had been severely injured in a jumping accident. After refusing a relatively easy jump several times, a friend of the horse's owner had insisted that the owner's horse was being temperamental and that the owner should make her horse jump. Even though a

72

little voice inside her told her that there was something wrong with her horse, she listened to her friend instead. (Scotty is healthy and being ridden today.)

For the **bones,** I stand at the horse's left side at his left foreleg. As the division between the cervical and thoracic vertebrae is deep within the neck, my right hand is about one to two inches above the withers, which is formed by the 3rd, 4th, 5th and 6th thoracic vertebrae and the cartilage extension of the scapula. My left hand lies across the outside of the left humorous. As the inside of the humorous lies inside the body, I will my etheric hand to wrap around the inside of that bone.

Shortly after Abez's death I worked on Sam, a 6-year-old thoroughbred who was off the track. Before Sam (and that is not his racing name) was 5 he had won $60,000. From the track, Sam's hocks in both back legs were bad, there had been an injury to the cartilage and muscles between the ribs on his right side, and the lower joint in his right front leg was arthritic from an injury to the bone in that area when he was 2. Racing or even riding a 2-year-old horse, when the joints in their legs are not yet locked, invites disaster. Sam's injuries are not uncommon for a former race horse. Sam was one of the bravest, strongest and powerful horses I had ever ridden. He took off even at the canter as though he'd been shot out of a cannon. If Sam had been able to win $60,000 with all those injuries, one has to wonder what kind of money Sam could have won if his original owner had waited until he was 3 to train him? My guides told me that he would have been a million dollar winner. What are your guides telling you?

The woman who had purchased Sam when he was 5 had bought him guaranteed sound, and wanted him for a jumper. When Sam came up lame, the vet took one look at Sam and told her that he should never jump him. She then let him sit for a year. The worst thing you can do for a horse with arthritis is not exercise him. When I began working with Sam, he had also been starved during that year of neglect and was over 200 pounds underweight.

Sam had never felt unconditional love. The first few times I worked on him in his stall while he was eating, he kept putting his ears back and looking at me. He was afraid that I was going to take his food away. For a bold horse, he was kind and gentle, but he was totally untrusting of humans. I worked with him on the touch points for bone, cartilage and muscle. I also rode him and taught him simple skills like stopping, bending when he turned, and to move away from my leg. Race horse owners and trainers have it in their heads that because there is a slight turn to the left at the end of the race, that race horses should only work to their left. This would be the equivalent of a bowler or javelin thrower only developing the arm that they threw with.

73

Modern exercise theory teaches us that we need to work both sides of our bodies equally, or there is a fundamental imbalance. The same is true for horses. There is no question in my mind that the first race horse owner that stops looking at his or her horses as commodities only, and begins treating their horses with love and regard will be truly blessed by the Creator. Sam worked for me because I gave him carrots, he felt love, and because his higher self wanted initiations into healing. In working with Sam and helping him to heal, I healed myself and my wounded heart.

For the **spine**, I move to the horse's right side. My right hand is just above the withers and my left hand moves as far down the spine as I can stretch. Jack, a 2-year-old gelding, couldn't walk without falling down. They felt that his problem was either wobbles, a central nervous system disorder, or trauma. As I felt the static in the aura above the spine, this was an indication that the problem was caused by an injury resulting in trauma. For Jack I worked the spine points, the muscle points, and the **nerve** points (just below the knee, which looks like the top of the leg). As he could barely turn his head to the left, I massaged the neck muscles. I pulled off and drained misqualified energy, and then filled the area with Light and colors. Since I didn't start working on Jack until several weeks after the injury, he was able to trot and canter after the 4th healing.

For the **tendons**, I stand on the horse's right side at his right foreleg. My right hand lies, from what looks like from the front, as the division between the leg and the chest. My left hand lies on the elbow joint and my fingertips lie across the humorous. Again I let my etheric hand drop into the horse's body. I am looking for the point where the biceps and triceps become tendinous. It helps to have a good comparative anatomy book, or you can simply let spirit do the work. If the **cartilage** is involved, I ask that the energy be directed there and visualize it working. In 1995 I discovered Pycnogenol which is from pine bark, and later grape seed (PCO) Phytosome (both products are available at health food stores) which helped heal the old tendon injuries in my upper legs. As the list of food items a horse is alergic to is longer than the list of things that he can eat, we must be very careful before giving any herbs or supplements to horses.

One of Abez's more dramatic injuries was not caused by a person. One evening I went to the barn and noticed a look of distress on my horse's face. After putting his halter on I proceeded to walk him out of his stall. I walked out, he fell out. Why? Because he had dislocated his left hip; and rather than moving forward, his left leg swung out to the side. He could not have come in from the pasture in that condition! What probably happened was that he was rolling in his stall and became cast (stuck). In trying to free himself he dislocated his left hip. I dropped the lead line and for well over an hour worked back and forth from the tendon/cartilage point, to the injured hip. I also used the pain drain and pulled off misqualified energy. At the point of injury I worked in the aura to reestablish the healed, normal pattern of a femur bone secure in the hip socket. Sometimes I did place my hands on the area. Again, one of the very nice things about an injury is that if you can get to it right away, dramatic results are possible. When I was through, Abez appeared more relaxed and he was able to get back in his stall. The next day the owner of the barn came out because he had heard about what had happened, but he couldn't understand why Abez was so active in his stall. We took Abez out and even trotted him a little bit. All I noticed was a slight hesitation at the left hip joint. Spirit told me to leave him in for a week, and then let him build up his strength in the pasture for a week. Two weeks after his injury, much to the amazement of everyone, I was riding Abez. He easily cantered, did side passes (movements to the side) and could do turns on his haunches.

For the **muscles**, I stand to the side of a horse at one of his hind legs. I place my hands on the insertion point of the gastrocenemus (page 76). My right hand on the left leg, left hand on the right leg. Or <u>to be safer</u>, I go from side to side and work on one leg at a time, beginning at the side where the involvement is (this point will be sore). Rather than jumping right in at the rear end of a horse, I let him experience the energy first at his neck or ribs. Horses have actually rolled their eyes back to look at me while I am working on them because most of them have never felt anything like healing energy coming out of human hands. When they figure out that the energy is making them feel better, they relax and oftentimes will go into a trance. In working with animals, as with people, I listen to my inner feelings. My gut tells me what to do.

Because they are work animals, and because horses are often worked at too young an age, injuries are the most frequent problems horses have. If there are other issues, I can adapt the same touch points I use on my human clients for my animals clients. If there is an issue with a major **gland,** for example, it would be both uncomfortable and unsafe for me to be half under a horse that near to his rear legs. On large animals it is easier for me to work with another healer. If there are two other people present, I can have either the owner, or someone else who knows the animal well, work on the opposite side of the animal's body (the other stays at the head and reasures the animal). I visualize healing symbols coming into my assistant's crown and out their hands. As with humans, I can also work directly over the affected area as well as with the touch points. With emotional issues on large animals and even smaller ones, it is easier to work on their back 2nd and 3rd chakras. **Fear** is held in the neck. The healer can massage the neck and then stroke the 'negative' emotion up and out. **Mental** issues can be addressed by placing the left hand over the 3rd eye and the right hand under the head.

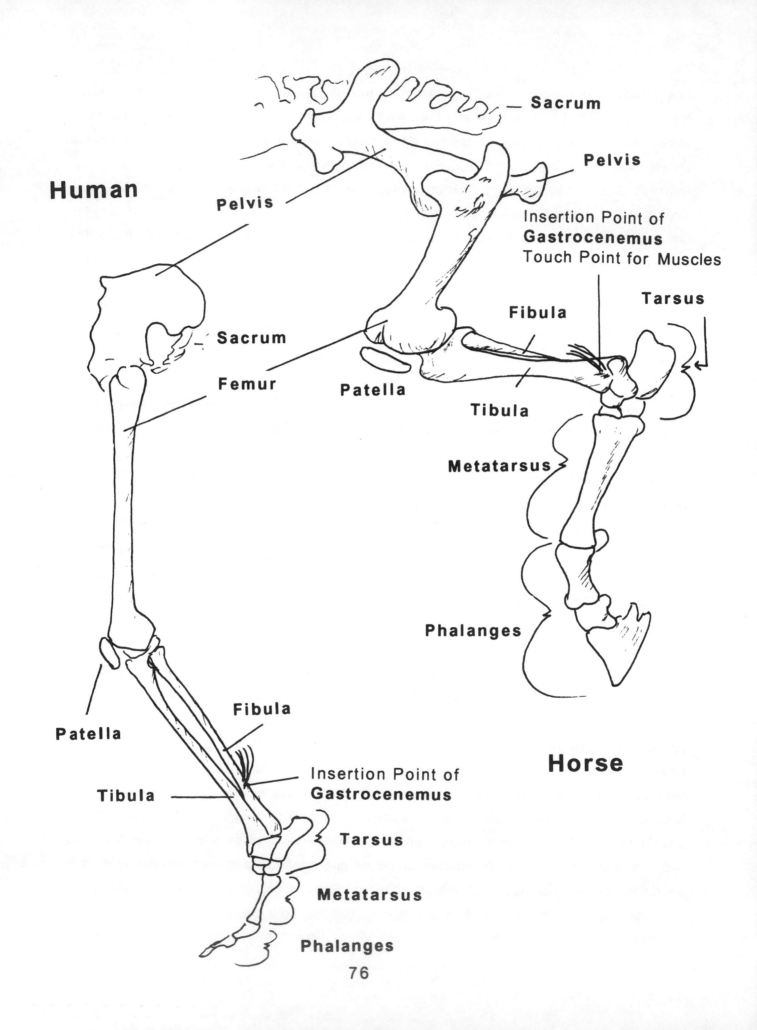

Human

Pelvis

Sacrum

Femur

Patella

Fibula

Insertion Point of
Gastrocenemus

Tibula

Tarsus

Metatarsus

Phalanges

Sacrum

Pelvis

Insertion Point of
Gastrocenemus
Touch Point for Muscles

Fibula

Tarsus

Patella

Tibula

Metatarsus

Phalanges

Horse

When an animal has had enough healing they let the healer know by moving restlessly about.

With animals as with humans, if they do not want to be healthy, if they are working out karma through their death, or if it is simply their time to go, the healing energy will help them with their transition. When my cat, Muffin, had to be put to sleep, I stayed with her so that I could comfort her, and so that she wouldn't have to die with strangers. We also do this for their protection. Bodies feel different after the soul has left. I saw Muffin's soul pass in front of me as she left her body and she gave me a gift. Your friends, relatives and pets will do this for you, too, after their passing. Newborns also bring in gifts for each of their parents. In order to receive these gifts we do not have to be cognizant that they are coming; however, conscious awareness always helps. We do, however, have to be open and compassionate in order to receive. At exactly the same time I had to have Muffin put to sleep, another woman I knew also had a cat with failed kidneys. She let him die on his own. I knew in my heart that her cat would be unable to leave her anything.

As an act of compassion I once attended the funeral of a client's father. Her family treated her miserably, and I felt that she needed someone there for her. The wake for the family was held an hour before friends arrived. We wandered the funeral parlor looking for the right room and finally found a small door. Upon entering, the casket was immediately in front of us, with the family looking on. As soon as they spotted us, everyone of this woman's family turned their backs on us and walked to the other side of the room. Later at dinner she was not invited even by her own son, to sit with the rest of the family. Sometimes I find it very difficult to stay out of judgement. While I couldn't see her father, I could feel that his spirit was very much present at the funeral, which was held immediately after the wake. I know he left my client a gift, and he generously gave me a very precious gift. However, when I tuned into my client's sisters to see if I could send them healing energy, I found that they were not only too closed to receive healing, but that they were not even able to receive what their father wished to bestow upon them.

I have had to forgive much in my life. I know to hold anyone bound is also to hold myself tied to this plane. As earth makes her quantum leap forward, I do not wish to be left behind on the wheel signing up for another 25,000-year reincarnation cycle on another 3-dimensional planet. One of the more interesting things Abez did after making his passage was to work through me in my dreamtime. For several mornings in a row I awoke with perfect recall of visiting and talking with Abez's former owners, and the owners of stables I had described previously. These dreams were as real as anything I have experienced in my life. In releasing them of their guilt, Abez freed himself.

77

Sometimes people will ask me if the grief I went through with Abez's passing was worth owning him. I have heard other people say after loosing a pet that they could never go through the pain of loss again. As for myself, I know and feel Abez's great joy and that he is still around helping me. I bless and thank Mother-Father God for the experience, which all of the money in the world couldn't buy. The time I had with Abez was more than worthwhile, it was unconditional love. While Dolores was doing the reading on Abez for me she told me that he allowed her to touch his left rear leg and he said to her, "Feel for a moment what it was like when the two of us were one." Individuals who are unavailable, who are emotionally and mentally incapable of taking care of themselves cannot be expected to take care of a pet or child. They miss the experience and unconditional love.

People will sometimes ask me during the question period after my lecture if they should give up eating red meat. I tell them that if their body needs it, or if they will be resentful if they do give it up, that they are better off eating it. We are evolving to a time and place where it won't be necessary or desirable. And I know that God will have other work for people to do who are now working in the meat industry. Nancy Moore and myself noticed that in society conscious New York, fur coats are becoming less and less fashionable. The benefits derived from animal testing have always been questionable. Now with high-tech computers, it is absolutely unnecessary and amounts to nothing less than torturing the helpless. Many different groups are asking for legislation to ban this practice.

The Church teaches that God's Energy is in everything. I believe this is true, and I know that we are all an expression of God and created in God's Image, not just mankind. Mankind for the greater part has forgotten to honor and seek the Wholeness. In the bible God gave man dominance over the animals. I believe that in Mother-Father God's Wisdom S/He charged the animals to serve mankind in order to help us to come back to the spiritual path. Kings and queens are supposed to serve the people. In the eyes of God all animals must be looked upon as royalty. When we show our love to animals, when an animal is able to receive human love, we in turn help them with their evolvement.

Who Are the Grays?
And Other Things that go Bump in the Night!

Earth, or Terra as she has been called in other times, is a three-dimensional world, where the Wholeness of the One is split, giving the illusion of duality. There is a Jim Henson film, <u>The Dark Crystal</u>, which explains this division in story form. It is a movie about a race of beings who through their arrogance broke off a piece of their master crystal. When the crystal split, they and their world tore apart as well. The master race then disappeared, replaced by two other races. There were those who used strength, "their hard and twisted bodies, their harsh and twisted wills" to control those weaker than themselves and to ravage the land. The second group were mystics. "Their ways were the gentle ways of natural wizards," those who work with, and have respect for the elemental forces. With love, but without power, they performed empty ceremonies, "numbly rehearsing the ancient ways in a blur of forgetfulness."

In higher vibrational planes we simply think and it becomes; thus, we miss the process of manifestation unfolding. We incarnate, or are born into a human body, so that we can learn and experience the nature of creation. Here time is fed to us moment by moment. It is in this manner that we can see the causal effects of our thoughts and actions as they come back to us. This is the nature of the living truth called karma. Karma is neither good nor bad, it is the way in which we learn to become responsible thinkers and co-creators with Mother-Father God.

We are also here to experience love. There are literally millions of people who have had near death experiences. Clinically dead, their souls had begun the journey home, to what is described as a wondrous, loving Light. If the soul's work has not been completed, it's sojourn is interrupted by spiritual mediators, angels if you will, who explain to the individual that it is in their highest interest to reenter the physical body. We do have free will choice, and in cases where the soul continues its passageway, death of the physical body is permanent. Those who come back to their body, and some do this even hours after a doctor has pronounced them dead. There is the story of the man who came back while his body lie in the morgue of a Catholic hospital. Wearing nothing but a toe tag he wandered the halls looking for clothes, a blanket or someone to help him. Of course, the first person he met up with in the hall was a nun.

People who have had near death experiences are able to relate conversations that occurred after their body and brain were pronounced dead by a medical doctor. They recount events that happened not only in the room where their body lie, but in far away places as well. Those who would have us believe that this is the only reality cannot adequately explain near death phenomenon in three-dimensional terms alone. The testimony of near death experiences is yet one more proof of the existence of other realities. Even though the testimonies vary, and any mental blockages can and do influence the information brought back, there is a worldwide similarity to the description of the phenomenon of the White Light on higher planes. As for those who see demons and come back into their bodies, being given a second chance, there are two explanations. First is that these are somebody else's thought forms, and in that case, they can easily be commanded to go away in the name of Christ. Laughing at them will also send them off. Secondly, these 'negative' entities were either worked with or created by that individual in his/her lifetime. In that case a healing is necessary, and as I have said before, it is easier to do this while in the body than after death.

The common message brought back by those who have had near death experiences is that we are more than our bodies, and we are here to learn the nature of love. We do this by opening our hearts to receiving love, and then compassion begins to flow from our hearts. We create beauty and harmony on earth through our hearts by being the mediators between what the Native Americans refer to as the power of the projective, masculine upper world and the loving, receptive, feminine lower world. In the Holy Kabbalah Hesed (love) joins with Gevurah (power) to form Tiferet (beauty and harmony). Regardless of which mystical or spiritual terminology we choose to use, our hearts are the center. From our hearts we hear Mother-Father God. It is in the heart that the expression of Mother-Father God flows from us.

When we get caught up in the games of a three-dimensional reality and we take ourselves too seriously, we begin to forget that there are other realities, who we are, and the bliss of Wholeness.

In opening out hearts we open our psychic abilities as well. Our heart is the key to unlocking the door to the way home, to what some call heaven. First, however, we need to find and create heaven here in the moment. Earth is supposed to be a vacation, not waking up to a nightmare every morning.

Because we have forgotten and have gotten lost in an illusion of duality, we have spiritual guides and angels who travel with us to help us on our earth walk. Those who can consciously communicate directly with their guides and the guides of others are called psychics. We are all supposed to have this ability. Jesus said, "You will do greater things than I have done." Well, what did Jesus do? He healed, bilocated (being in more than one reality at the same time), he loved and treated everyone as his brother, he manifested, prophesied and he spoke directly to

Mother-Father God and to his guides and angels. Many saints were able to do these same "miracles." Spiritual abilities are looked upon as extremely remarkable achievements outside of our ordinary ability because we have lost contact with other realities. Supernatural means that a particular event is beyond explanation in terms of the known laws which govern this material universe. The laws of this reality are not the same as those governing other realities. What is impossible here is common phenomenon on other planes of existence.

When we become enmeshed in a three-dimensional reality and forget to seek the Wholeness, we begin to create illusions in a veil of tears. Let pain bring due reward of love and Light seems to have been the motto of the Piscean Age. One high drama is the story in the Old Testament of the fallen angels luring man into the pits of hell. The good news is that God gave Lucifer and the third of the angels who fell with him only a short time to tempt man and their time is ending now! In all great past civilizations there existed a common prophesy, the coming of a great golden age, a thousand years of Light, love, peace, joy, illumination, fulfillment. A return of the golden age of the angels. If man so chooses the time can be extended for another thousand years. (I cast my vote now for prolongment.) Aztec, Mayan, Egyptian and Incan calendars are coming to a close now. Even the Australian Aborigines' calendar came to an end August 1987, the month and year of the harmonic convergence, when all of the planets lined up. The Piscean Age is over and quite literally "this is the dawning of the Age of Aquarius." The song that was written over two decades ago is about to become a reality. Earth is in the process of changing roles, she is moving from serving as a repository for the working out of undesirable thought forms into a premier position in this universe. Another planet will serve as a kidney for this universe.

Those who have worked out their emotional and mental issues, and have been willing to learn their lessons will, if they so wish, move into a golden age of which no earthly words can begin to describe the magnificence and splendor thereof. What makes this particular transition especially remarkable is that this time we are taking our healed, whole, youthful bodies with us into higher dimensions. **But** we must be willing to do the work now.

As earth moves up in vibration, everyone who is going into the Golden Age will begin to resonate to increasingly higher and higher frequencies. We begin to get glimpses of this phenomenon when initially crystals disappear and then are found in places where we have already looked a hundred times before. Then this begins to happen with other objects. These "things" are vibrating back and forth between dimensions. What we don't realize is that we are vibrating as well. We don't remember because if the wonder remained in our conscious memory, we would not want to stay here to finish the work that must be done. However, some people are beginning

81

to bring back brief visual patches of beautiful colors. This is the future sending back the reality of this grand new world so that we have a clear vision of the future with which to pull ourselves forwards with.

To be able to vibrate into the golden age one needs to be unshackled from what we refer to as negative thought forms and destructive emotional patterns. Those who don't, won't go! There is a big interest in alternative medicine these days. Masking symptoms with drugs and surgery without getting to the core issues behind the disease and pain prevents the physical and other spiritual bodies from vibrating at the necessary higher levels. More and more individuals are involved in spiritual practices, discovering the knowledge of their oneness and then honoring All There Is. As earth moves up daily in vibration, as people are healing, as people renew and reconnect with their own spirit, as Mother Earth is again honored, the veil between the third and fourth dimensions gets thinner and thinner. More and more people are getting in touch with other realities, the gift we refer to as psychic abilities.

The physical is actually where you are. The difference is that on higher levels of vibration, form becomes less dense and more easily manipulated. Thus, on the fourth dimension beings can shape shift or alter their appearance more easily than you and I can change our clothes. Rumor has it that an interesting cast of characters exists on the fourth dimension. The credits include: Spirit guides, earth-bound or what some call lost souls, nature spirits, angels (both celestial and fallen), and extraterrestrials (both beneficial and malevolent). As we become open to our psychic abilities and the fourth dimension, we need to know who it is we are addressing. This is important! Lucifer is the "father of lies," and there is a very simple way for us to know the Truth. <u>We are not supposed to blindly follow auditory psychic messages!</u> This is not trust; this is insanity! If you hear a message from another reality, ask **3 times**, "In the name of my Lord Jesus Christ this is so?" Or ask, "In Divine Truth this is so?" Or ask, "In the Light of Christ this is so?" Or ask, "In the Love of Christ this is so?" If you see a life form from another dimension, question it. Ask **3 times**, "You have come in the love of Christ?" Or ask, "You are in Divine Truth?" Also, "Kadosh, Kadosh, Kadosh, Adonai Sebayoth" translated means "Glory to God in the highest" will send negative thought forms running. The "big names" or the "heavy hitters" work! The Mayan name for God is Kunaku. Yes, that works! If the message or messenger is not in the Truth, then it or they have to go.

<u>Just because someone says that they are channeling a master, archangel or famous person does not necessarily mean that it is so</u>. While Mother-Father God may have allowed Lucifer to tempt man, S/He has not left us without resources. We always have the right to know the Truth.

Repeating one of the above statements, or something similar, **3 times** works on a conscious level, in meditation, or in the dreamstate. You then wait to see if the vision holds or if the message stays. If it is not in Truth it has to go! God is like the good school teacher or the good government, who doesn't have lots of rules, but rather a few good ones.

Some people find that it is also helpful to have a positive affirmation signal in their own body. Human bodies are our earthly vehicles and are like computers. The owner of the body should be the one who gets to do the programing. A series of classes designed and channeled by Dorothy Espiau called "The Gems of Excellence" self-programs a series of tap/touches using different number combinations on the body. For example, to clear: Start at the head of the fibula on the outside of the left leg, circle clockwise with coned fingers of the right hand and say 2-3. Move half way down the outside leg, circle and say 5-3. Move down to the ankle, circle and say 6-5.

You can program your own **positive affirmation signal** simply by asking for one. This is done quite easily in meditation either in a group or individually. If it is done within a group there is the added advantage of the power of the group effort. It is helpful to have one person facilitate. Facilitators can serve to both hold the energy and to guide the experience. If they have their own positive affirmation signal, they serve the additional role of teacher. The advantage to working with a teacher, or one who is already doing what you aspire to do, is that by working in the teacher's auric field the student is able to make quantum leaps. Process is accelerated.

To begin, sit in a circle and make certain that everyone involved in the process is clear. If everyone is not clear, a simple exercise to do is to cone the fingers of the left hand and circle counterclockwise 3 times over the heart chakra (over the thymus) and saying 3 times, "eight-seven-three-one-two to release horror." Then cone the fingers of the right hand and circle clockwise 3 times over the heart chakra and say 3 times, "eight-seven-three-one-two to integrate God's Love." It works because we are tapping into Sacred Geometry. This simple exercise shows us that we really are in charge of our lives.

Your positive affirmation signal can come in a variety of different ways. The woman in Ireland, Ann Wood, who taught me this, has a positive affirmation signal whereby her head turns to her right side after she asks three times if the psychic message she received is in Truth. Other people have a vision that they see in their third eye, or a twitch, or a energy current. It is actually our own higher self and our angels who decide what is the best possible signal. If you do not get it on the first try, try again. Ask that it come in loud and clear. If you do not personally like the signal you get, then ask for another signal. We do have choices! After receiving the signal, ask three times, "In Divine Truth this is the best possible positive affirmation signal for me." All that is written here on these pages remain interesting ideas until we experience other realities. Receiving a positive affirmation signal in ones own body is certainly evidence that there is something else out there.

If you also want a negative affirmation signal follow the same procedure. The advantage to having a negative affirmation signal is that after asking three times if the spirit or message is in Divine Truth, we have either the confirmation of yes or no. We can also ask our angels to bring these signals in loud and clear so that there is no confusion or doubt. Ask and we really do receive!

One indication that we are not clear is when the confirmations we receive are conflicting; that is, we ask and it is yes one time and no the next. We become unclear when we get stuck in our own negative emotional or mental patterns. When we are in judgement of others, we get caught up in their "stuff." To feel sorry for someone comes from the mind and is in fact a judgement; to have compassion comes from the heart. One way to stay out of judgement is to simply view another's action as being a very interesting way for them to remember who they are. Unconditional love means loving people where they are, and allowing people to be who and what they are. It is not up to us to give unsolicited advice or to try to change people who do not ask for help. Do we have the right to steal someone's lesson? What if we are the ones who are wrong? Do we have the right to steal someone's gift? Morality is taught through example, not by preaching. This does not mean; however, that we should allow harmful behavior to be acted out in either our front or back yards. There comes a time when we call a halt to the games!

Dowsed messages should also be checked out verbally three times. Dowsing and kineseology work because the physical body has a consciousness. The best dowsers, however, are 85% accurate because fears and our own self-interest can influence the physical body even when we think we have consciously put our brains into neutral. Because our bodies hold a consciousness, psychics who work with police departments on murder cases actually go into the morgue and touch the dead body to get psychic impressions that the body is still holding. It will do this for about 7 days after death. To prevent their minds from getting in the way, these psychics typically do not want to know anything until after they have completed the initial reading.

In **dowsing** or kineseology the important thing to remember with asking questions is that they should always be put in the form of a statement. That leaves the pendulum or body free to decide the validity of the statement. Secondly, be as specific with questions as possible. Third, remember to ask about all the alternatives. For example, you may get a yes swing with the pendulum on possibility A, but you may get an even greater yes swing with the pendulum on possibility B.

Dowsing begins the same way as when asking for a positive affirmation signal. Make sure that you are clear. Hold the pendulum with the thumb, index and middle fingers of either hand. Focus on the crystal. Then ask out loud three times for your best possible Universal yes.   When the pendulum begins to move, check it out by asking three times, "In Divine Truth this is the best possible Universal yes for me." Do the same for no. My yes moves outwards from my body, back and forth; my no moves from left to right, from side to side. If there seems to be some confusion or if the issue is still unknown, my crystal moves in a circle. I know a woman whose yes is any movement of the pendulum, while her no is no movement what so ever.   Another common movement of the crystal is clockwise for yes, and counterclockwise for no. If you use a crystal for dowsing, remember to clear it as you do your other crystals; either in sunlight, in cold water or place it on a clear crystal cluster.

If you work psychically with physical objects, be they pendulums, Ouija Boards or in table tipping, it is extremely important to keep checking to make certain that the messenger, the message and the object you are using are clear. Again, you do this by repeating 3 times, "You have come in the name of Jesus!" when the pendulum, Ouija or table starts moving. And after each and every question is answered ask, "In the name of Jesus this is so." If the board is not clear, you will receive conflicting answers. Clear and allow underlings the opportunity to go to the Light, to be free from their constriction. I do not send them to a black hole, they are already there. There are many ways to clear, there is a very nice one in An Ascension Handbook by Tony Stubbs on page 95. I have included the Hosanna clearing in the chapter on symbols Pages 116 and 117).   The longer a fourth-dimensional underling and their messages go unchecked, the stronger hold they have. When this occurs, what the Catholic Church calls an exorcism is required. This was the message of The Exorcist, we are better off staying away from psychic phenomenon than to jump in not knowing what we are doing.

Whenever we provide a way for what we call "negative spirits" to return to the Light, the blessings and beneficial energy Mother-Father God sends back to us for this human act of kindness is beyond measure. When I work with entity clearings on objects or individuals I give the underling the choice of leaving the planet or going to the Light. As we have freewill choice, I must accept that there are those who do not want to go to the Light. I cannot force anyone or

85

anything to be subjugated to my will, even if my intentions are the very best. If I do so, I must suffer the consequences of my decision. I know one woman who does clearings and forces underlings into the Light. Yet, she does not understand why it is that she herself cannot stay clear.

Sometimes in releasing black magic the energy is insistent, and it is in divine order, that it go back to the <u>central core of origin</u>. I persist in expelling negative thought forms. They must leave! If, however, the individual I am working on murdered that soul in this or another lifetime, then that entity feels it somehow has a right to inflict pain and suffering. I then work with the earth-bound spirit and explain that s/he is imposing as much harm on themselves as they are on their victim. In New York I worked on a friend of Charlotte's who felt that she had a fallen angel attached to her. I worked on her for over an hour while my spirit guides untangled him from her. All the while he mocked me. When I told him that Mother-Father God had forgiven him long ago, he continued to ridicule me claiming that he wasn't interested and that I was a fraud. My guide, Straight Arrow, told me that he was frightened. So I asked him, "Is it true? Are you afraid that God really hasn't forgiven you?" With that he broke down in tears and fell into the arms of Jesus, who said, "I have been waiting a long time for your return brother." The angels asked him to drop his old robes, which reeked of a vile odor, and were then burned. Afterwards they dressed him in clean garments. Then he went to the Light.

I tell my students, "It doesn't matter whether or not you believe in the Grays, there will be people who will come to you who will claim to have been abducted by spacemen. Your refusal in not accepting their experience as valid is not going to help them to heal. You must work in your client's reality."

There is a story that is told of the Grays which would actually make a popular science fiction movie. They are gray in color with large heads and eyes, emaciated limbs, and small mouths. This is actually their space suit. Their brains are insect-like, and their skin is scaled like a reptile. They have suction-type disks on the tips of their fingers like an insect, and they leave behind a sticky substance on whatever they touch. (A flaw in the cloning process partial manifests in the inability of a clone's ring and little fingers of both hands to fully function. These 2 fingers lie over the palm when the other 3 are extended.) Their second (creative) chakra is shut down, so they are devoid of emotions, but they do take pleasure in anothers fear and pain. They fit Andrew Vaachs' definition of evil like a glove. They have shut down their heart chakras, so there is no heart love energy. People who have heart problems have a gray pallor to their skin. The choice of color in their space suits is an interesting reflection.

The Grays come from a twin star system where the suns are so close together that early in creation life forms in each solar system began to telecommunicate by use of mental telepathy. They advanced their psychic abilities from there and went on to form a highly developed civilization. The mass accumulation of gold and money for the purpose of controlling others was never of interest to them. They perfectly understood that with knowledge, both psychic and technical, comes power. It is this power that they used to subjugate others to their will. What their intellect and reasoning missed completely was that knowledge is not finite; the process of creation is ongoing. In cutting themselves off from the Creator and formulating a god to suit their own selfish purposes, they closed themselves off to Wholeness, Oneness and Truth.

Those individuals who have had abduction experiences say that the Grays tell their captives that their kidnapping and subsequent violation were something that they agreed to before they were born as part of their life's plan. We have to ask, how would the Grays possibly know our personal agreements with God? Are there such things as inappropriate agreements? Is this an acceptable defense in any known court of law? We are here to learn to love and respect one another, and also to stop being victimized.

Eons ago the Gray's form was humanoid, they very much resembled us. Initially the Gray's decision to reproduce by cloning served the dual purpose of convenience and control. Later cloning became the only way to propagate the species. As their distorted thought forms brought about their own physical deformity, along with it came the inability for any of their kind to reproduce naturally. Reproduction is neither a loving nor a natural act. They are a dying race! Their demise was predicted 2,000 years ago in the Apocalypse, for they are the beast that the 7-headed beast worshiped as gods.

The psychic energy that they are drawing upon is what keeps their distorted bodies functioning. When the pool of psychic energy runs dry, the Grays will no longer be able to stay in their present bodies. If it would be possible for them to change forms at that point, they would loose the greater part of both right and left brain knowledge they have gathered. The Grays stand as an example for the rest of creation; that is, what we do to others really does come back to us. We cannot harm another without inflicting something worse upon ourselves.

The Grays paid a high price to exert their will over God's Will; they quite literally lost their souls and unevolved to a condition of group consciousness. The eyes, the window to the soul, are a lifeless black void. Personality, what little there is of it, does not survive death. If there is any remaining vestige of emotion, it is the jealousy they hold for humanity because we do have individual souls. They think that they are here to send all humans packing so that they can have the golden age for themselves. In Truth these creatures cannot steal our inheritance. If they had only read Saint John's <u>Revelations</u> they would know why. John has a list of folks who quite simply are not going into the golden age (murderers, kidnappers, thieves, etc.). This is not a judgement but rather a fact. Some thought forms do not belong in higher dimensions to pollute the rest of creation. Kindergartners do not belong in the high school chemistry lab! Lessons are meant to be worked out within certain parameters on three-dimensional planets. That is, there are people on this planet and the Grays themselves who think that they can despoil, ravage and pollute Earth; then leave for a millennium, and then return to a beautiful planet and have the golden age for themselves. They are like the hyenas in Walt Disney's <u>The Lion King</u>. This thought is contrary to **All** Sacred and **All** Natural Law.

In this drama those people and groups, in both the private and public sectors, who work with the Grays do so in exchange for the development of their own psychic abilities. In this soap opera the problem for these folks is that the psychic abilities they have been given by the Grays are only an illusion. What the Grays are actually doing is psychically projecting their thought forms, the ones that they want their receivers to perceive. How's that for a Universal joke?

There is another mystery in this play. Since the heart is the gateway to the upper chakras; and as the Grays' hearts are closed, access to the higher chakras is also closed. They have shut down their emotions, so their second chakra is not active.   That leaves the solar plexus, naval, meng ming (chakra at the small of the back), and root chakras only. Where is the psychic energy that they are using coming from? The Grays are operating out of the remembrance of their own group mass consciousness, a time and place when they were highly evolved. Since the energy in that pool is not being replenished, not only are they a dying race, but their psychic abilities are coming to an end as well. Since the Grays cannot get to or even past their crown chakras, they totally lack the ability to transfer psychic or healing energy from Mother-Father God to anyone. When the Grays lose their psychic abilities, the people who think they are working with them will lose their illusion of their abilities as well.

More good news is this. In working within my client's perception, I suggest that they either visualize or ask their angels to bring and surround them with the color cobalt blue before going to sleep at night. Some of my clients go so far as to surround their whole homes with cobalt blue. <u>Cobalt blue dispels fear both through its calming influence and its ability to reveal Spiritual Truth. It's true, "The truth shall set you free." The abductions stop and my client is left in peace!</u> As simple as this is, it works! I have had clients with previous abduction experiences call me to say that they woke up in the middle of the night and saw the Grays on the other side of an aura of blue color. The Grays could not get through it! At this point my clients do not ask if the Grays have come in Divine Love, they say, "In the name of Jesus go." The Grays leave, and the kidnappings are halted. This is how powerful we truly are! Anyone can ask for cobalt blue in a conscious, unconscious or dreamstate. Egyptians and Mayans painted the ceilings of their temples blue to keep unwanted influences out, not to imitate the color of the sky (the temple floors were not painted brown or green). Asking our angels for cobalt blue before going to sleep at night makes our dreamtime more peaceful and productive.

We need to know that we are safe, as well as ways to protect ourselves before developing our psychic abilities. Once we 'get it', when we know we don't have to be afraid of anything, when we release and heal the torture chambers we created in our own minds, when we understand that we truly are powerful co-creators of our own lives, when we understand that we are not transient but are the power of being that is eternal, then we can begin to use the other 90% of our brains that we do not use. It is at this point that we can use both our right brain (creative, psychic) and our left brain (technical, resource centers) to become responsible, loving co-ceators with Mother-Father God.

We expand our consciousness, connect with the God and our true selves by meditating, which is going within to achieve a state of Love and Beingness. When we transcend ordinary consciousness, when we have our own direct experience of knowledge of self, we can align to our life's purpose and become self-realized. The same events occur in the lives of those individuals who are stuck in fear-based personalities and those who are self-realized. The difference is that the first group misses the joy and passion of life, which is deeper than the pleasure-pain wheel. When fear comes up in new situations, they clutch or flee. The second group recognizes fear in change, and looks for the adventure in living life moment by moment and then experiences the journey of life when events are taken step by step. Erhart Vogel, author of Self-Healing Through Awareness of Being, is one of many teachers who teaches self-realization through meditation. Both Vogel and Osho (Ragneesh) teach heart-centered meditation. The heart is the gateway to the upper chakras, it is where we listen to God, it is the avenue through which affluence flows into our lives, and it works in conjunction with the 3rd eye so that we can be self-realized. Erhart Vogel states that when we are self-realized, our mind, feelings and emotions are in syncronicity with who we are. When we are connected we realize our potentials. Dick Roberts has been aiding people in career/life transformations by helping them to discover their true passion, hidden talents, and life/career purpose. When we have a sense of direction and there is meaning to our lives, we are on an evolutionary path. Depression,

89

anxiety and addiction occur when we are living outside the potential of who we are. Dick Roberts has an audio tape series called <u>Discover Your Life's Work</u> which consists of two tapes: "The Joy Experience" and "Aligning to Your Personal Vision". These tapes help us to make choices with confidence in the 'battle ground' between personality and self. When we lack knowledge of our true self, the personality sees fear (which will always come up whenever there is change) as something to be avoided. This fear-avoidance strategy also prevents us from living and doing our life's work in joy and with a sense of passion. Fear then stagnates our entire growth. When we are self-realized we know that we can succeed in our chosen path.

One additional thing some people do for protection is to put themselves in a pink bubble in the morning. Pink represents the higher vibration of love which is compassion. Also, when our 'enemies' come into our consciousness we can bless them and say "Go with Jesus! Go in Love! Go now!" If we need to, we can keep repeating the statement. Initially we may have to make more of an effort and say this several times. If we have learned our lessons from these people, who are also our teachers, and sometimes our best teachers, they will go.

Black serves as a vessel to hold the Light. If it were not for the contrast of the dark side, the light would not shine in the illusion of duality. Also, without the black brotherhood we would have no motive for moving onto a higher expression of a reunited Mother-Father God.   At the end of the movie, <u>The Dark Crystal</u>, when the master crystal is made whole again, the two races rejoin and are made whole as well. "What was sundered and undone shall be whole, the two made one." A part of our own healing process involves looking at what we call our own dark side, those lifetimes and events in this lifetime that we all have that we are not particularly proud of. We don't even know that what's lurking in our hearts is that, like Alec Baldwin in <u>The Shadow</u>, "I cannot forgive myself for the evil I have done." When we let love and Light into our hearts and souls, there is forgiveness, acceptance and Oneness. To do this we need to stop doing battle with ourselves and the God within us. We need to make peace with God and find the magic within us. By embracing and loving ourselves totally for being human as S/He does, we can forgive ourselves and others. It is in this state of total unconditional love and acceptance that transformation and healing can take place. Then we realize that everything has been, is in, and always will be in Divine Order. We know that we are and always have been a necessary part of the divine plan. It is in this state of consciousness, joy, love and bliss that our psychic gifts become a vehicle to take us home to True reality, to Wholeness. In a state of Wholeness we are the limitless power of being that is eternal.

Psychic Abilities and Healing

With an understanding of the fourth dimension, we are now able to work on the development of psychic abilities. Along with each of the physical 5 senses (seeing, feeling, tasting, touching and smelling), there is a corresponding sense that perceives on other dimensions. We lose what we do not use. Since we have not used them for so long, in order to open these centers we need to utilize appropriate meditation and concentration techniques. We always create what we focus on, but the paradigm is that forcing our wills actually shuts down these psychic centers. What is required is gentle, loving, persistent attention.

There are as many ways to meditate as there are groups that promote it. Meditation has long been an important aspect of spiritual practice and soul growth. The Catholic clergy, popes, sisters and brothers alike, meditate. It is best, but not necessary, to do any kind of meditation on an empty stomach. Prior to meditating, <u>focus and breath into</u> stretch exercises or those that open joints (shoulders, elbows, wrists, hips, knees, and ankles). It is important to remember to do any movement exercises in both directions for balance. Several of my teachers do eye exercises as well; that is, rolling the eyes clockwise and counterclockwise, moving them back and forth, and up and down. These eye exercises are good for the physical eyes as well. My Aunt June, who does these exercises regularly, is in her 70's and neither wears nor needs glasses.

After exercising and before meditating, it is helpful to ask for the assistance of angels or guides. If I have a specific intention in mind it is beneficial to state it out loud before I meditate. Intentions should be clear, yet at the same time allowing Mother-Father God to take care of the details. Grounding before meditating is also important; common ways in which to do this are to see or feel the etheric (light body) feet, or the root chakra going deeply into the earth like tree roots. Some people surround themselves with White Light before meditating. To further open the third eye and crown chakra, before beginning I slowly tilt my head back so that the top of my head is parallel to my spine. Holding this position for less than a minute, I then gently bring my head back to an upright position. (*If you are prone to neck injuries, crushed vertebrae, etc. this is not something you want to do. Check with your doctor first before trying this, it is not for everyone.*) Once in a meditative state in order to go into deeper levels, I pray to go further inward, I take a slow, deep breath, exhale and relax. When I am through meditating, I pause and watch all of my chakras spinning clearly. I see my intention flowing out my root chakra and into the earth. Then I move excess energy down to a center that is roughly 1 1/2 to 2 inches below the naval where it can be stored; this can be done through visualization or feeling. Then I give thanks and gratitude.

Many people through different schools are taught the use of silently repeating a mantra. The mantra often is a word meaningless in itself alone. Many people use Ohm, and Amen (pronounced ah-men) works as well. Effortless repetition occupies the left brain, and with a corresponding slowing down of the breath, the intuitive right brain becomes active, that in turn leads us to the silent observer within. If it is effortless repetition, other thoughts can come in and when we become aware that the mantra is no longer being repeated we gently go back to repeating the mantra. If the mantra alters on its own, we go with the flow until it feels right to go back to the original mantra. When we enter the silence of the Great Mystery within us, we remain there until our conscious mind brings us back. If a pain comes up in the body, repeating the mantra into the discomfort can release it. Relaxing and breathing into the center of pain is a proven technique for moving through it. This technique also works for fears, for in moving through fear we can see what is on the other side of fear. Repeating the mantra into other 'negative' emotions works as well; rather than keeping them bottled up, we watch to see where our breath and the emotion carries us. If visuals come in, enjoy them without trying to figure them out.

Silva Method utilizes both visualizations and in some cases, corresponding body movements. The original name for this workshop was Silva Mind Control, which conjured visions of brain washing. What the word 'control' was meant to convey was that we are supposed to be in control of our thoughts, and with our imaginations we can literally change our lives. If you begin with Silva, it will lay a foundation for the rest of the psychic work that you do. If you finish with Silva, it will tie together everything else, all of the other classes you have taken and books you have read. Silva Method has aspects of self-hypnosis. Another one of my students, Roxanne Louise Miller, has written Your Unlimited Potential, a full self-hypnosis course and guide to creating yourself and your life through use of your mind. Teri Mahaney, Ph.D., author of Change Your Mind/Life, teaches people how to create their own meditation tapes.

Arhats is a word for the consciousness of ascended beings. Arhatic Yoga utilizes the breath in combination with different mantras and visualizations in meditation. In Taoism the word Tao means God. However, God is not a noun, but rather an active verb; a creative, dynamic, thinking, invincible force. The Taoist's Microcosmic Orbit in another fashion also combines both the breath and visuals in meditation. The more advanced meditation includes mantras at each of the chakras as well.

East Indian gurus teach several meditation techniques. One is to focus on a particular chakra of the body. The mantra is similar to the sound the breath makes. On every inhale we say to ourselves, "So", and on every exhale we say to ourselves, "Hum". If you wish to try this, close your eyes and sit with spine erect. Relax, let your thoughts go, and allow your breath to naturally slow down. Begin repeating the mantra, "So-Hum", starting at the crown in coordination with your breath at least 3 times. Feel the prana or Universal energy being drawn into the chakra on every inhale and the expulsion of used energy within the body released on every exhale. Then begin to be aware of the silence at the top of the inhale and bottom of the exhale where there is no breath, where there is no mantra.

There is a vertical energy line that originates from Source and runs down through our crowns, and out the root chakra. It grounds at a chakra that is located about 12 inches below our feet, and continues down into the earth. The crown chakra at the top of the head spirals upwards; the root chakra at the base of the spine spirals downwards. The other major chakras are connected both front and back to this vertical energy line. At the point of connection to the vertical energy line, the diameter of the chakra is quite small and increases in size as it spirals outwards towards the surface of the physical body and into the aura. We have a chakra at the third eye and the back of the head, front and back throat chakras, front and back heart chakras, front and back solar plexus chakras, naval chakra and one at the small of the back, and front and back creative chakras.

After repeating "So Hum" at the crown, the mantra is repeated down the front chakras to the root chakra and then up the chakras on the spine. Maintaining **focused concentrated attention** on each chakra as we breath and repeat the mantra; aware that the chakra is breathing along with our breath, and of the gap at the top and the bottom of the breath. Upon reaching the crown, visualize Light and pause for a few seconds. Repeat the mantra starting at the crown, only this time I work down the spine and up the front. (This direction cleanses the chakras.) At the crown, repeat the entire process and this time working down the front and up the spine. If you do this meditation it is important to begin and end with the energy moving <u>down the front</u> and up the <u>spine</u>. **Or** you can do the process entirely by moving the energy down the front and up the spine, and if the energy starts running too fast, reverse the direction of the energy flow by moving down the spine and up the front.

If you would rather say another mantra, Amen (pronounced ah-men) or K'in (Mayan word for Sun pronounced key-yin) work well. Many people simply say Ohm. This is the mantra I began with before I took any classes. Repeating a mantra , allowing it to take its own form apart from the breath, is yet another meditation method. Some meditators prefer staying focused on the Light coming into the crown

An advanced meditation is to sit in meditative silence with no mind, no thoughts for at least one minute. We can get into this place by simply repeating a mantra and gently allowing it to become or not to become what it will be. Another technique is to try to hold one visual image for one minute with no other thought. The goal of these particular meditations is to reach the silent observer within, which is the point of our own creation and creative powers. Try these meditations if it feels right to do so. For until you actually experience nonordinary reality or a past life, my words will remain only mental concepts. The key words to remember in meditation are **persistence** and **patience**.

With practice of this meditation the kundalini, the energy of the root chakra, will begin to rise. Several teachers including Master Choa Kok Sui say that the kundalini is actually awakened from the crown downwards, not the root chakra upwards. With the meditation I have just described, the lower chakras are cleansed before the fire rises and reaches the brain. They say three things are possible when the fire reaches the brain - insanity, death or enlightenment. We want door number 3. By clearing the lower chakras first, enlightenment is then possible. Master Mantak Chia, and Taoist masters teach us how to circulate the energy of the kundalini up the spine and down the front central meridian. It is an involved process which Mantak Chia calls the microcosmic orbit. To either slow the orbit or utilize the energy for cleansing, bring the energy of the kundalini up the front and down the spine. In addition to moving energy down the front and up the spine, there are mantras (chants) and mudras (hand positions) that can be incorporated into the meditation. An example of a mudra would be the thumb touching the little finger. We often see Jesus depicted holding his fingers in this position. If you wish to try this while you are meditating, one at a time, touch your thumbs to different fingers (possibly beginning with the index) and see for yourself the different energy patterns you can create.

Good teachers are always a good investment. You not only receive proper instruction; but when you are working and studying in the aura of a teacher, you are able to make quantum leaps forward. Before investing in any teacher or workshop, I check out to make certain that this is the right teacher for me. Our guts tell us, if we would only listen to our instincts. Jesus has lead me to many teachers on this earth plane. He has no desire to take total responsibility for my spiritual growth, that would be possession. Any true guru guides his/her disciples to finding their own guru within. Any organization or individual who claims to be the only one with the answers, doesn't! Jesus taught his disciples to do the same things he could do, and they in turn were given the authority to go out and teach. The original New Testaments contain this knowledge and were intended as a gift for humanity. Remember the story that Jesus tells of the

94

stewards, and of how the steward who buried his master's wealth was not rewarded but rather reprimanded?

This meditation will help you to surrender to your guides, angels and your own godself. Before beginning this meditation visualize yourself in a pink bubble and fill it with cobalt blue color. To open your third eye and crown, tilt your head backwards and hold for a few seconds. Bring your head back to an erect position. On every exhale say to yourself the word, Ohm. Slow your breath naturally. Concentrate on both the mantra and the silence at the bottom and top of the breath. If visuals come in, enjoy them without trying to figure them out. When you are proficient at this, see a White Light at your crown just inside your head. Maintain **focused concentration** on the Light. This Light is real and will bring energies of healing, knowledge and illumination. If you wish to enhance this or any other meditation further, take a crystal in each hand; left hand up and right hand down. The points of the crystals facing towards your body. In this way you will not only benefit from the crystal's energy, but you will set up a circle of energy around you. Another meditation would be to maintain focused concentrated attention on the crystals in your hand. As crystals, like everything else, come from Mother-Father God and have a consciousness, they can teach us. Remember to clear the crystals when you are through in either cold water, sunshine or on a clear crystal cluster. In the crystals' efforts to assist us, they may absorb some of our negative energy.

In utilizing visuals in meditation we should not manipulate the free will choice of others. If we choose to do so, that misqualified energy will come back to haunt us. Some salesmen, for example, are taught to visualize a particular individual or business buying their goods or service. This projection is interfering with another individual's right of choice. Later the salesman wonders why the sale didn't hold, or the commission didn't come through as promised, their job is lost, etc. The true use of the third eye is to pray with our heart for a specific thing without tying God or spirit down to particulars. For example, if we need a place to live, ask for the best possible home. Then in silent meditation watch with the 3rd eye and wait for the answer.

This is not to say, however, that you cannot use particular visual techniques. For example, before going out on a job interview, send blue color to the building and room you will be interviewed in. If this is the best employment for you and you are to meant to get the job, you will; and if there is something better for you, you will be saved a whole lot of time and trouble. There are other techniques that are nonmanipulative. A simple check is: If we wouldn't want somebody doing it to us, then we shouldn't be doing it to somebody else!

95

The other caution with utilizing visuals is that it may not be addressing the core of the problem. For example, we can visualize fat cells being burned up, or fat literally wrung out of the muscles; but if the emotional issue behind the unwanted fat is not healed, our own subconscious or superconscious will either recreate the fat or create something else to call our attention to the problem. Visualization is also neither a substitute for exercise nor for eating properly.

Shaman journey work also utilizes visuals. Before there was meditation, before there was hypnosis, there was the shaman's drum. It is the rapid, pulsating, nonvarying beat of 205 to 220 beats per minute which quiets the active left brain and sends the shaman into altered states of consciousness. The overtone of the drumming harmonizes and balances the two hemispheres of the brain, and may be the reason why in this particular form of visualization, we feel dissociated from our bodies and participate in our imagery. It is more powerful than virtual reality.

Our awareness resides inward in our seat of consciousness. Our seat of consciousness is in our bodies when we are awake and travels when we are asleep or if we are in certain altered states. For example, our sleeptime is our soul's awake time. It is then that the soul leaves through the crown chakra and travels outside of our body, connected by a silver cord which is mentioned in many different mysticisms and spiritual texts. Our brain is a computer, it is neither us nor our souls.

In shamanic journey work the shaman is always in control and may return to 3-dimensional reality at any time. With spirit guides and helpers, s/he is always protected. The hot words right now are "body-mind connection." In shamanism the missing element, spirit, completes the formula, body-mind-spirit connection. Before beginning journey work one traditionally needs to honor the 4 directions and 4 elements, and call in spirit helpers and guides. In both magic and shamanic work it is necessary to set a goal or an intention before beginning. Goals may be as simple as finding a power animal or spirit helpers, or exploring aspects of nonordinary reality. Common needs are for healing, knowledge, strength, new guides and wealth for the accomplishment of various ends.

We use different states of consciousness during our waking day. For example, when we speak with a friend, testify in court, or if we are working at a computer, we are not in the same state of mind. Just as there are various levels of awareness and concentration within an earth plane trance state, there are also multidimensional levels of awareness in nonordinary reality. In general there are three worlds that shamans from different cultures around the world travel to:

The lowerworld of power animals and nature spirits; the upperworld of the angels; and the middleworld which appears to be closest to our three-dimensional reality. Michael Harner in The Way of the Shaman refers to this range, which is beyond our ordinary perception, as nonordinary reality. To the larger aspect of ourselves this realm is real reality. With knowledge of the Truth, we humans are supposed to be focused in a joyful way in physical reality, with the flexibility to explore other realities. These are the same realities that the hero experiences when, with super-awareness, s/he follows an inner knowing and courageously, without question does whatever is required in the moment. Nonordinary feats of bravery and daring are accomplished in altered states. The senses are heightened in what is described as a peak experience. Whole audiences can be drawn into other realities while engrossed in a well-orchestrated play, concert or sports event. When the actors, musicians or players skillfully draw our attention in, we focus intently on the event and physical reality disappears. In this state the audience is taken into heightened awareness and given glimpses of other realities.

Nothing but our own fears and negative thoughts can harm us in nonordinary reality. Nothing! Spirit helpers, guides and angels are there to assist us. By an act of sheer will, we can resist or send anything 'negative' away. Even our own or someone else's fearful projections can be easily banished through laughter. Drug induced trances rarely if ever reach higher states of real reality, and the would-be journeyer is always at mercy of the drug.

Once in New York I had two men call me who wanted to learn Reiki and other rays of touch healing. One of the men told me that he used to do drugs on a regular basis until he had one extraordinary experience. He went into the higher realms with the real celestial angels. He stopped doing drugs, turning instead to advanced meditation techniques attempting to recreate the experience. They took my classes and initiations, and they were supposed to wire my fees to me when they returned to Germany. They didn't. I learned a lesson, and my guess is that this particular man is still trying to contact the celestial angels. If we are to go into the higher realms, we must be responsible. As Jesus said, "If you cannot be trusted with the small things of this earth, how can you be trusted with the keys to heaven?"

Our effectiveness in nonordinary reality or any other type of visualization is entirely dependant upon how much spiritual or healing energy we hold. To acquire strength and powerful spirit helpers, Native Americans would go on vision quests. The only difference between a hero and a coward is that the hero walks through his/her fears. For their acts they were rewarded with the same elemental healing rays that I have been describing to you. Other ways to become strong psychically are to go through personal trials, living and speaking our truth no matter how difficult or impossible it appears at the time, right action and conduct, experiencing love and other virtues, meditation and traveling to places of power. Initiations into Reiki and the other rays of touch healing is also a way to channel energy. However, without correct intention and responsible conduct this energy can be easily lost, for in this lifetime Mother-Father God has promised that these spiritual forces will not be debased. The misuse and abuse of Sakara and the forcible manipulation of Sophi-El was responsible for the sinking of Atlantis and bringing Egypt to her knees. This abuse of power will not be allowed now!

Some individuals are born with healing or psychic abilities, and catch on naturally because they have been involved in spiritual practices in other life times. However, there are no shortcuts! Anytime someone hands you something on a silver platter, it's probably tin.

Using the third eye to visualize can be learned by anyone. One very old exercise is to hold a simple object like a pencil or crystal in front of you, close your eyes, and hold the image as long as you can. Look again. Try to hold more of the details. Maintain focused attention. Look again. Try to hold the image longer. Do this for 5 minutes a day. It takes 21 to 30 **consecutive** days to build a new skill or change a habit. At the end of 30 days work with another object and you will find that it does not take as long. Then sit with a mirror and try to hold the image of yourself in your mind's eye. Your next step would be to ask to see yourself in your perfection. You can also call your guides and angels in to work either on or with you, depending upon your need. An old Wiccan method for opening the third eye is to stare at a burning candle flame for one minute and then hold the image in the third eye. With this particular technique, if you start to get headaches, stop using the candle or meditate on the candle for a shorter period of time. Use another object instead and go back to the candle when you feel that you are ready. There are also some wonderful guided meditation tapes and meditation classes to aid you.

One way to develop psychic hearing is to listen to the tone carried after ringing a Tibetan bell. Or listen after striking an ordinary bell. If you wake up early in the morning, listen to the wind. It can be a powerful experience. The Holy Inquisition burned people alive for this act alone. Remember to check out your messages! People who hear on other levels of reality do so not with their physical ears, but hear about an inch and a half above the ears at the temple bone. If thought is coming from higher realms, the vibration enters through the crown and then processed in the brain so that it becomes understandable to us. Thus, the length of time since the spirit's last incarnation is not a factor in communication. In your meditation ask that these centers be cleared and then watch your spirit helpers clean the area. It is also important to give ourselves permission to see and hear on other levels of reality.

Each of our physical senses has a corresponding psychic center. Yes, we can even smell and taste in other realities. Clairsentience is the ability to feel on other levels and enters through the solar plexus. When the Truth is spoken and every hair on our body is standing on end, we know it is the Truth. This is an aspect of clairsentience.

Clairaudience is the ability to hear clearly on other dimensions. Messages are heard just above the physical ears, just inside the skull. Psychic messages come into the brain, are translated into language, and then processed through the master pituitary gland. That is why the sound seems to be inside our heads. Higher beings communicate with us through our crown chakras.

Clairvoyance means to see clearly. The vision of our inner mind corresponds to the third eye chakra. The third eye is comprised of 2 chakras; one between the eyebrows and another at the forehead.

Inner knowing comes in through the open crown chakra. It is this information that we can trust. However, this voice is so quiet that our minds must be free of the incessant chatter and clutter. Freeing ourselves from the negative, worn out audio tapes we play about ourselves, and the 'old bad movies' we keep rerunning brings peace of mind and the ability to listen.

It follows then, in order to open these centers we have to be able to get quiet and then meditate on the points mentioned previously - crown, pituitary, solar plexus, third eye, and the points just above the physical eye. There are several things we can do to increase the effectiveness of our meditation: 1) The Taoists understand the healing power of smiling into our organs; we can also smile into our chakras. 2) The heart holds the key to developing our psychic abilities. We can open our hearts to love and allow love to flow into these centers. 3) Call upon our guides and angels to assist us. 4) Check out all messages and messengers three times. "In divine Truth this is so?" or "You have come in the Light of Christ?" We follow our own hearts wherein lies our own inner Knowing and Truth; we are not supposed to blindly follow auditory messages and beings from other planes or planets.

It takes 21 to 30 consecutive days to establish a new habit. It is probably wise to work on one attribute at a time, but if you have the time and are guided to work on them all, by all means, go for it. For example, if we want to open the eye of our inner mind, for 30 consecutive days we would meditate for 30 minutes a day, smiling and maintaining focused concentration beginning with the heart and going on to the crown, pituitary and third eye.

To see past lives, stand in front of a mirror, a bathroom mirror will do. A cobalt blue background, if you can arrange it with a towel, sheet or shower curtain, is preferable. Hold a small candle in between you and the mirror. Focus your attention on your eyes and watch your own past lives flip before you. This is possible because we are vibrating. Einstein proved that time and space do not exist the way we perceive it. Everything is happening simultaneously. At first you will see the faces change. As your skill develops, you will see costume changes. If you have a group of people, a fun parlor game is to have someone stand against a blank wall (again, if you can do it, cobalt blue is best) and dim the lights. Focus your attention on the individual's eyes and watch as the past lives flip in front of you. Initially you may have to half close your eyes. As you get better and better you will begin to see in lighter and lighter environments. I ask those present during such a session to verbalize what they are seeing, and it somehow helps others in the group to see as well.

If there is a healer in the group other things are going to be happening. What I have found is that people who are flipping rapidly are actually integrating their past lives, experiences and wisdom. For those who are changing form more slowly, those past lives that are coming up are coming up for healing. No matter how handsome or how beautiful they may have been, if there is a negative thought form present, their faces will look sickly or have some kind of distortion. In some cases death wounds will be visible, or they may be holding onto a weapon. At an angel conference after doing the third eye initiation for a group, we practiced seeing the past lives of one another. One of the women present, who was one of my students, had done this exercise with me on Long Island almost 2 years previously. On Long Island a Native American brave with half of his face blown away appeared. She personally was not in any kind of pain, although the past life was angry, distressed and in obvious discomfort. At the angel conference the brave reappeared; however, much healing had transpired since his initial appearance. The form was more illuminated, stronger, and his face was completely restored. Not everyone in the group sees with the same definition, clarity and completeness; for example, not everyone sees the body and clothes change. A few of the people present at this particular session saw the brave complete with colored war paint on both sides of his face.

Why had this past life been in distress? There can be many reasons. Traumatic deaths can hold the soul earthbound. All great mysticisms teach that the soul has three days after death to go through the thought forms and emotions they created in life. If they are too heavy, the soul cannot go to the Light and remains earthbound. In the case of this brave, it felt as though dying in a state of anger and hatred held the soul in bondage. There is a difference between protecting yourself and what you love, and killing with animosity or thoughtlessness. It was very difficult

100

for many Native Americans, who honored and respected earth and creation, to understand the total disregard and destruction of nature by most white Europeans. <u>Dances With Wolves</u> touched our hearts and opened our eyes to the truth. With their mystical and spiritual practices, the Native American nations or tribes had at their disposal the means of defeating the white man, even though the Europeans had guns, but their loathing and contempt interfered with their spiritual abilities and practices. The Native American deaths, however, were not in vain, the shedding of their blood into the land insured that this nation would always be spiritual.

Traumatic deaths can also result in the soul's immediate reincarnation. Because time and space do not exist the way we understand it, it is possible for these anguished souls to reincarnate in the same birth year. They bring into the second life much of the memory from the first. There was a woman who claimed to be the daughter of the assassinated Russian Tzar. Observers claimed that not one of the royal family could have escaped. Yet, this woman, while unable to speak Russian, could recount things to her grandmother that she couldn't possibly have known unless she was a member of the royal family. She was the Tzar's daughter, the reincarnation of the Tzar's daughter. Men who are killed in battle, such as Viet Nam, and are unable to move through the trauma and go to the Light often immediately reincarnate.

Manifestations of misqualified or unresolved thought forms from past lives appear in the present life in the form of pain and disease. When the past life is healed, the present body is healed. In some cases this means the healing of more than one lifetime. When I did this initiation at Ishpiming, a new age retreat center in northern Wisconsin, one of the men kept flipping between Native American lives and white European settlers. What made his past lives particularly interesting was that the bone structure and features were always similar to his present incarnation. In reincarnating back and forth between two clashing groups, by walking in another's moccasins, the soul sees perceived differences and learns to love. In his present life as a white male practicing Native American ways, he is resolving, loving and harmonizing past conflicts.

One man I used to date had alternate lifetimes between being a black slave and being a slave trader. He told me that in pictures taken of him in his youth during the summer when he was tan, that he looked like a little black boy. Others have gone back and forth between being burned as a witch, and clergy of the so called Holy Inquisition. Today in the Middle East many souls are going back and forth, as they are in India, between different religious groups. Initially many people do not want to see this at all! We do not like to look at lifetimes that are in discord with who we are now. However, by embracing all aspects, loving our dark sides, and cultivating and integrating love and power within us, we become whole. If we could only see that in this and any other lifetime we can only do what we are capable of doing in a particular space and time. Also so much is dependent upon what we have come in to experience in a lifetime. What we perceive as tests come from our own higher selves. There is no such thing as failure, simply an understanding that more growth is needed before we acquire mastery.

If there are healers in the group viewing past lives, they can also ask to see the current body on the most basic levels. That is, specifically, one at a time ask to see the skeletal, cardiovascular system, etc. To do this focus your concentration between your own eyebrows while visualizing. When asking to see on higher levels, concentrate on your forehead. The colors you see through the forehead will appear brighter than those you see when you use the eyebrow center. At the eyebrow center you will see forms. When you can use both the eyebrow and forehead centers together, you will perceive forms that have more dimension and more color than those objects and people that you see in a 3-dimensional reality using your physical eyes.

When our subconscious mind is in conflict with our present reality, we become upset with our subconscious. We think the subconscious is illogical. In truth the subconscious is as logical as a computer. Meditation in this instance serves another purpose: First, problems arises when our old inner programmings do not fit changed perspectives. For example, childhood or adolescent sexual abuse results in the adult thinking that love has to hurt or it isn't love. This is in definite conflict with having satisfying loving sex. Meditation can help in the process of releasing past harm and in reprograming new constructs. Secondly, problems arise when our mind is given conflicting paradigms or programs. On the one hand we are told that we live in an abundant universe, on the other we are presented with fears of lack and limitation daily. I know many people who simply do not watch the nightly news anymore. We do not need to have recessions or depressions in our lives if we don't 'buy into' the negative programming. Thirdly, our own superconscious may come in and reprogram the subconscious as our life goals change. Our meditation can let us know when we have to switch gears. Fourthly, we can find and correct inversions, omissions, distortions and misfiling. Meditation can help sort through muddled confusion and get to the truth.

The Silva Method helps create in the inner mind a laboratory where a male and female guide council and work with the meditator to get to the heart of the issue, and to create. It is a good class and I found it extremely helpful. We each in our own minds can create an inner sanctuary, a place to meet with our angels, guides and our own higher self. It is here where we find our inversions. For example, we subconsciously believe love is hate, so we draw in harmful

102

relationships. Or perhaps we have misfiled information in our subconscious. For example, we have filed joy under pain, so we attract accidents and mishaps. In our inner sanctuaries we can find our denials. For many of us it has been denying love to ourselves that has caused the greatest grief, for in not loving ourselves as God loves us, we create misconceptions about Him/Her as well. In seeing the inversions, misfiling and denials for what they are, we can reprogram our own subconscious.

Sorting out the truth not only helps our mental and emotional state, but with a quiet mind our psychic abilities are enhanced. Without the confusion and the constant chatter we can be more observant. As all psychic observations are viewed through the mind and feelings of the psychic, when we unclutter our thoughts and emotions, we become clear channels or receivers for psychic impressions. Clear psychic information aids the healer in facilitating the healing process.

I have found that the visuals my guides give to me are directly influenced by their own incarnations. For example, Abez's thought patterns and the visuals he send me are very much horse orientated. Once I saw a woman's past life in which she was a man who was blocked. I asked Abez, "How is he blocked?" (*Yes, it is important to ask questions about the information we receive psychically.*) Abez showed me tangled bridles. I tuned in. My inner feeling and knowing then told me that this man had a twisted perception of control and that he had misused power.

I cannot emphasize enough how important it is for the healee to verify objectively, and/or ask for confirmation on the information that the healer or reader is bringing into the session. Even so-called advanced psychics need to verify that the messenger is indeed who they say they are and if the messages are in divine Truth. We can also verify for ourselves the information we receive in our meditations. When Dolores Arechavala did the reading for me on Abez, she suddenly looked quite startled. I have learned to pay attention, and I asked her what it was that she saw. She hesitated and then said, "You and Abez were once wild horses together. It is what he loved, freedom." I immediately saw myself as a white mare, and without telling Dolores what I saw, I asked her what color I was. She answered, "White." A week later I had left Los Angeles and was in New York. It was late at night and I was lying in bed neither asleep nor awake. In this state my arms were lengthening, my shoulder blades were shifting, as was the rest of my body. I had the sensation of using my front limbs as well as my back limbs to move forwards with. My soul was remembering what it was to be a horse. With awareness I came back to consciousness. My body shifted back. It took me awhile before I could fall asleep.

As I began to open more and more psychically I made certain that I took enough potassium for my nerves, for it is the nerves that carry psychic energy. To protect my thyroid, I took minerals. While vitamins are best taken with food, it has been my experience that minerals are best taken with water on an empty stomach at night before going to bed, which also helps me to fall asleep (although initially it is a little hard on the stomach). Chelated (bonded) and coloidal (liquid) minerals tend to be more easily absorbed by our bodies than metalic mineral tablets. In taking vitamin capsules I make certain that the covering is digestible and not plastic. With minerals it is difficult but not impossible to find an absorbable multimineral supplement with no added vitamins that contains the 60 necessary minerals we need daily in correct dosage. <u>Trace mineral means that our bodies need minimal amounts of these substances</u>.

We are more than our bodies; however, we do need to take care of them. Joell Wallich was a veterinarian before he became a medical doctor. He is an author, and in 1991 he was nominated for the Nobel Prize. He applied the agricultural health care system (preventing and curing diseases in animals with nutrition) to his human patients. In the early 1960's he was hired through a 7.5 million dollar government program to do autopsies on zoo animals who died of natural causes. In approximately 17,500 autopsies Dr. Wallich found that these natural deaths were in fact due to a nutritional deficiency. When animals lick the ground or crib (gnaw on the wood in their stalls), or when we continually crave sweets or chocolate, these are some of the signs in which the body is trying to say that there is a mineral deficiency. The average life expectancy of a medical doctor (the majority of whom do not believe in vitamin and mineral supplements) in the United States is 58 years, considerably lower than the 75.5 year national average. Granted that doctors as a group have an unusually high suicide rate; however, Joell Wallich says in his lectures that many of them die from diseases that farm animals, who do have a supplemented diet, would not die from. Dr. Wallich said that he took up a hobby while speaking around the country; that is, collecting obituaries of doctors and lawyers. These obituaries back up his statements. Dr. Wallich has an audio tape available through Toddy Minerals, which I believe is called "Dead Doctors Don't Lie". What can I say?

Poor diet and lack of vitamins, minerals and trace minerals in our pesticide-herbicide-chemically grown and produced foods may also be the reason why our children are performing so poorly in school. The bottom line may be that we may all need to supplement our food intake. Angels can and have performed miracles, but we as healees are expected to participate in our healing. As healers, the healthier our bodies are, the stronger the healing energies can flow through us. It is a part of the process in becoming clear and conscious healing channels.

Symbols and Their Use

Symbols are the conscious communication of subconscious minds. The Holy Ghost speaks in symbols. Symbols have long been used in both magic and divination. Everything comes from Mother-Father God, everything has a consciousness. Symbols function because they, too, have a consciousness, and they know and are able to go about and do their work. Symbols are held in God's Consciousness. For us to try to determine the cultural origin of symbols entraps us in linear time. God breathes symbols out and they are made available to us. It is up to us to be conscious to them and be willing to work with them.

We all have the ability to work with symbols. Some people are born with healing energy and some of those people may also carry the ability to work in a dynamic way with healing symbols. As with hands-on-healing, the more healing energy the healer is able to channel, the more effective the symbols will be. The ability to work with symbols can be learned in the second initiation into Reiki, which also further opens the crown to the healing ray from element earth. Afterwards, in the class the initiate is typically taught 3 Reiki symbols and how to use them. In using symbols in healing, we utilize our psychic abilities.

Since Sai Baba and other higher beings retrieved the missing Reiki symbols and information, my students and myself have reinitiated and taught Reiki Masters from all of the associations and branches thereof. Karyn K Mitchell, author of <u>Reiki: A Torch in Daylight</u>, reinitiated a large group in South America. Gallina Molodtsova in Moscow has reinitiated many European Reiki Masters. What they, and other students of mine, and myself found out rather quickly was that there is no core body of information concerning these symbols, even within the same Reiki organizations. The symbols' definitions, what they are able to do, and how they work is entirely dependant upon the Reiki Master from whom one takes the second and even the third Reiki class.

The ascended masters do not think in terms of better or best, only what is. What I am about to share with you is knowledge that Sai Baba and other higher beings have shared with me on the inner planes. There are symbols that either do not work or will not work as well unless you are initiated into them. Since much of the information about how to use Reiki symbols is applicable to other symbols, I have included examples of these as well. And there are symbols herein that you will be able to use. When people say that healing symbols do not work, either they have not been initiated into them or they are misusing them. There are also healing systems such as Angeliclight for which there are <u>no</u> symbols! Like aromatherapy, Angeliclight works with vibrations in an altogether different manner than Reiki, Sakara or Sophi-El do.

While drawing any symbol, there are things that I can do to further empower that symbol. First, rather than using just my index finger to draw, I cone my fingers. Thus, using not only all of my fingertip chakras, but the palm chakra as well. Second, I draw with both hands, not just one. Third, after drawing the symbol and saying its name out loud while I draw it, I repeat the name 2 more times. Thus, saying it a total of 3 times, the number of creation. Fourth, Eileen Gurhy found that punching (poking the symbol after it has been drawn with coned fingers) will further empower it. This technique works for other symbols as well.

These two symbols are both called **Cho Ku Ray**. I draw the clockwise Cho Ku Ray with my left hand, and simultaneously draw the counterclockwise Cho Ku Ray with my right hand. Clockwise connects to the heavens, or what the Native Americans call the projective masculine energy. Counterclockwise connects to the earth, or the receptive feminine energy. Together the balanced energy works to energize all other symbols. They can be drawn in front of a symbol, after a symbol, or a symbol can be sandwiched in between two sets of Cho Ku Rays. Most people who take the second Reiki class have been taught the counterclockwise Cho Ku Ray only. My Reiki Master, Margarette Shelton, gives her students the knowledge of both Cho Ku Rays.

This Reiki symbol is **Say Hay Key.** It looks like the sphinx or a horse's head. It is good for mental healing, but not exclusively so. When we change our thought patterns, our emotions often heal as well. When we alter our thoughts or our perception, we alter our lives. This symbol is also taught in second degree Reiki classes.

Zonar was the first of the symbols Sai Baba gave to me. I draw the "Z" first and then come up and draw infinity three complete times. Zonar works well with past life and karmic issues. Valerie Weaver was given that infinity is a Reiki symbol which works on emotional issues. Our cells can carry the memory of trauma, both the shock of our own individual experiences and those of the mass consciousness.

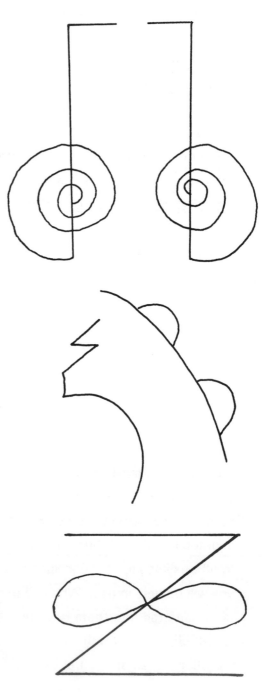

106

Whether or not you believe in reincarnation, whether or not you were one of the 11 million people burned as witches, we all own a share of the trauma within the mass consciousness. This holds true for all holocausts, as well as all individual crimes. What we do to another, we do to ourselves. This is a holographic universe, the same divine energy flows continuously through each one of us. Each part contains within it the consciousness of the whole. Interestingly, Zonar is also the symbol used by a secret metaphysical society called the "Z's" at the University of Virginia. Benjamin Franklin, who wrote The Farmer's Almanac, which is based on astrology, and Thomas Jefferson were both deeply interested and involved in metaphysics. Thomas Jefferson designed the architecture for the University of Virginia.

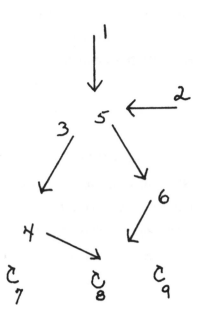

Harth is the second symbol Sai Baba gave to me. For many people, this is their favorite symbol. It stands for love, truth, beauty, harmony and balance. It is a powerful symbol for the heart as well as from the heart, from which healing and love flow. After drawing the symbol and energizing it with Cho Ku Rays, close your eyes and you may see a 3-dimensional pyramid constructed to scale rotating in front of you. Envisioning ourselves going into the pyramid in meditation can be a powerful experience. If you are so impressed to do so, in meditation see yourself going into the symbol Harth. *(This techniques can be done with other symbols as well.)*

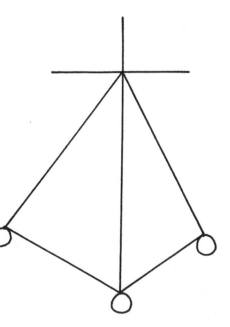

One of my students in New Jersey, Aaron Sapiro, met a Japanese American, who as a young boy left Japan with his family just prior to World War II. Before leaving, his family had worked with some of the men Mikao Usui had trained as teachers. The family had been given the symbol of a cross with a pyramid in the middle of it by these healing teachers.

The third and last symbol taught in most second degree Reiki classes is **Hon Sha Za Sho Nen**. It is presented as the absentee healing symbol. While Takata gave out two versions of Dai Koo Mio, the master symbol, she gave out approximately 15 different versions of Hon Sha Za Sho Nen. Within each one of the versions there are variances. Sai Baba told me that Takata had made up the symbol and that it was a combination of Buddhism and Hawaiian shamanism. One time I had a Buddhist monk take my class. He told me that there was Buddhist chant, "Hon Sha Za Sha Nen", to help release Karma. Interesting! There are no coincidences. This particular version of Hon Sha Za Sho Nen I am showing you encircles the individual or the issue and brings up the root cause by squeezing it out.

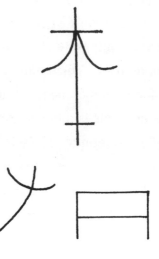

Mara is a Reiki symbol which connects and grounds us to the Earth. Originally it was given to me in a different form and called Rama. The 5 spirals represent the 4 directions and 4 elements. The spiral in the center of Mara represents our heart. Our hearts are the center of the medicine wheel, the center of the circle. The 2 "v's" coming together within the center represent the feminine and masculine aspects of God Him/Herself. When this symbol is intoned Mara, the straight lines shift and begin looking like ley lines on the earth's surface; while the spirals form a vertical energy line between heaven and earth, with the central spiral intersecting the point where the 2 lines converge. I invite you to meditate on this phenomenon for yourself. Mara is very good for people with no earth in their astrology charts; it helps them to ground. In the second Reiki initiation, this symbol opens the chakra that is in the sole of the feet, which further opens the initiate to the cobalt blue healing energy of Mother Earth and the blue-green energy of the sea. As it is of the earth, it is also a symbol for prosperity.

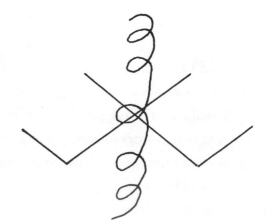

Halu is the third and last Reiki symbol that Sai Baba gave
to me. I give it out in my Reiki III classes, but have decided
to include it within this text because I believe that it was
never Sai Baba's intention that these symbols be sold alone
for large sums of money. It is Zonar intensified. The tall
pyramid is for mental healing. The so called tall, pointed
dunce caps that they used to put on mentally slow children
actually worked. However, by referring to them as dunce
caps, much of the beneficial energy was negated. The
infinity in the middle of Halu is for emotional healing. By
closing the "Z" the energy is enhanced. Besides healing,
this symbol can be sent to our meditation rooms before
meditating. Harth, both Cho Ku Rays, and Halu are a
powerful healing combination. Halu is drawn in this
manner. I start by drawing Zonar, saying Zonar 3 times
while drawing the infinity symbol. I lift my finger and
close the "z" from top to middle. Then I lift my finger
again and close the "z" from bottom to middle. I draw the
tall pyramid and say Halu 3 times. I draw the circle at the
top, which represents the cap stone of the pyramid,
ccunterclockwise. We must be initiated into this symbol
by someone who has been initiated into this symbol in
order for it to work.

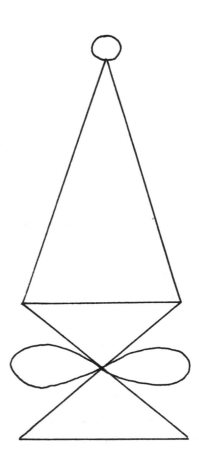

Symbols were so secret that in the past Tibetan monks would draw them with the tip of their
tongue on the roof inside of their mouth when doing healings in public. Symbols were so guarded
that while the teacher would draw symbols for the student, all paper was burned after each and
every lesson. In our present time period God has promised that divine energy and the symbols
themselves will not be misused; thus, everything including sacred texts and sacred symbols are
coming into the Light for us to look at and evaluate. I have energized all of the symbols drawn in
this book. If you would like to feel their energy and use them in your own self-healing, simply
place your palms on the symbols. To further activate the energy, get into a meditative state and
direct healing to wherever it is that you need it. The symbols will keep working no matter how
many times you use them if you will remember to give thanks to the symbols *(like everything
else that comes from God, they too have a consciousness)* and the angels who work with them.
Without gratitude and honor, we all run into a dead end with our healing.

Each of the elemental rays of healing has what is referred to as a **Dai Koo Mio**. It is this symbol when used in correct combination with 3 other specific symbols which will open the initiate to the full expanse of the energy. The energy transfer is made by an individual who has been initiated, knows the initiation procedures, is able to bring down, hold and transfer the full expanse of the ray. We cannot initiate people into something that we ourselves do not have! This is why I suggest to people that they check out their potential teachers and their students. Takata gave out only two Dai Koo Mios. It is the hard-edged Dai Koo Mio, not the gesture drawing (which has the same number of strokes) which "holds the key" to full empowerment into the healing ray from element earth. When we began to reinitiate Reiki Masters from other associations, we consistently found that while Hon Sha Za Sho Nen was a theme in variation, those Reiki Masters who had the hard-edged Dai Koo Mio all had the same identical symbol, stroke for stroke. Susan Peterson Seigler worked with a Tibetan monk in the early 1970's before he returned to Tibet and was subsequently murdered by the Communists. He had shown her both Dai Koo Mios and told her that the hard-edged version was the stronger of the two. Eventually, in one way or another, I receive confirmation on all of the information Sai Baba gave to me. As a further affirmation, Susan's monk showed up for her initiation.

As all of the Reiki Masters know that they cannot do the same healings that Usui and even Takata could do, they all know that something has been left out. Some of them have altered the Dai Koo Mio in an attempt to raise the energy. One Reiki Master gives out a different Dai Koo Mio every time he teaches the class. Another Reiki Master has translated Dai Koo Mio into Japanese characters, not realizing that the symbol, like the energy, comes from God, not Japan. And it doesn't come from Tibet either! Each of these people are serving their purpose, walking their path and finding their own way home. What I invite my audience to do wherever I speak is to experience and check out the healing energy first hand from the Reiki Master and their students as well before taking Reiki classes from anyone including myself.

Richard Bennett and Joel Pfeiffer were given the same message simultaneously during their Reiki Mastership initiation. Their insight has consistently been affirmed by psychics; that is, the Dai Koo Mio is only to be used for initiation, not healing. It does and will work in healing; however, the healer then assumes responsibility for the healee's healing. This is the last thing anybody should have to do. We have enough just being responsible for ourselves and our own actions. I personally was never impressed to utilize this symbol in healing after I became a Reiki Master. It would have been foreign to do so. For those whom I am reinitiating as Reiki Masters, who have been using it for healing, I tell them that it is like the innocent who walk into the medicine wheel incorrectly, a state of mercy and grace is given by the Creator.

110

Shanti (Peace) is a symbol channeled in by Pat Courtney of Milwaukee, Wisconsin. It heals the past, which allows us to live harmoniously in the present, thus releasing the future. Shanti can be used for manifesting the best possible.

Sati was given to me by Lawson Bracewell of Punskaiki, New Zealand. The equal arm cross represents the equal quality of Spirit (mother-father, male-female, etc.). It represents the four directions and four elements, and it is the same cross that Jesus worked with. The Romans were the ones who elongated the lower arm and turned it into the object of his crucifixion. Jesus never meant for us to venerate the implement of his torture and death; instead we are supposed to honor the elements and forces of creation. The 2 interpenetrating masculine (clockwise) and feminine (counterclockwise) circles represent the dynamic relationship of the 2. Out of this union the manifestation of Mother-Father God, as well as the soul on earth, will be greater as we come out of the age of darkness and into the Age of Aquarius. Sati can be used in the healing process for the opening, integrating and balancing of the male and female aspects so that the individual can live joyfully, harmoniously and lovingly in reality. In a very short time it will no longer be, "As in heaven but not on earth."

To draw Sati, I start at the top of the equal-arm cross and draw a mirror image of the cross only. I lift my fingers and place them on the center of the bottom line of the rectangle, and again draw mirror images. Then I simultaneously draw the 2 interpenetrating circles, one clockwise and the other counterclockwise.

111

Fire Dragon is a Yoga symbol. It is indirectly a symbol for the kundalini in that the 7 swirls represents the **7 chakras**. It is drawn from the top down. Works well with spinal injuries. Moves energy up the spine by addressing issues and removing blockages in the chakras. For example, in the second chakra it can aid women and men who have either gone through, or who are going through menopause.

I stand corrected! **Johre** was brought in by Iris Ishikuro, one of the 22 Reiki Masters Takata initiated. Before her death, Iris made Reiki Mastership available and affordable. Johre is White Light and this symbol connects us to Earth's guardians. I have found that it works particularly well on releasing blockages. To empower a symbol I say its name 3 times, in instances such as this where a symbol has 6 characters, I find myself saying the name Johre each time I draw a character for a total of 6 times, <u>a multiple of 3</u>. Often I give my students visuals to help them remember. You may use mine or make up your own. From the top down there is the number 7, a clockwise spiral going in, a check mark, a fisherman's hook, an up-side-down cross, and a clockwise Cho Ku Ray.

Motor-Zanon is a minor Sanskrit symbol that at least one Tibetan monk uses for exorcisms. It has two names and works to release viruses in this manner. Energize the symbol with Cho Ku Rays and intone "Motor" 3 times. Motor goes into the body, and the little squiggle in the middle rotates on the horizontal line, catching the virus. To help the symbol change polarity (which it will eventually do on its own) draw and energize the same symbol and call it "Zanon" three times. The symbol reverses polarity, leaves the body and takes the virus with it. This symbol does work with AIDS. However, the root problem with AIDS victims is most often extremely low self-esteem and self-hatred. <u>These and other core issues</u> <u>behind any disease or pain must be addressed first before</u> <u>real healing can take place</u>. Whether it is AIDS or some other disease, there are individuals who love their pain, or the attention it brings. Some people simply enjoy wallowing in misery. If they want to be healed, for them the question is, "Why are you doing this to yourself?" and then finding aspects within them that can be built upon to establish a true sense of feeling good about themselves. Many people who have been HIV positive for years and have never gotten AIDS owe this to their spirituality. Spirituality means not only loving Mother-Father God, but realizing that God is within and loving ourselves as well.

Valerie Weaver, M.D. has been given a number of symbols by her guardian angel. I'd like to share three of them with you. **Integrate** is for integrating the shadow side into ourselves, for unifying love and power to form beauty and harmony within. It is also for the consolidation of new knowledge or energies.

Gratitude is the symbol for Universal thanks. It may be sent to Father-Mother God, angels, etc. at anytime or in ending ceremony. One of the ways we begin disconnecting from God/Goddess in any golden age is when we take but forget to give thanks. For example, many of the vortexes like Sedona are losing their energy because people come there to take and do not give back. This is not the manner in which the universe works. The strongest force is love, but close on its heals is gratitude. When we give thanks we complete the cycle so that more can be given to us. When we forget to give thanks we stop the cycle. This symbol may be sent to anyone or anything. This is the symbolic representation of the gesture of thanks with the arms crossed over the chest. The circles represent the elbows and closed fists.

113

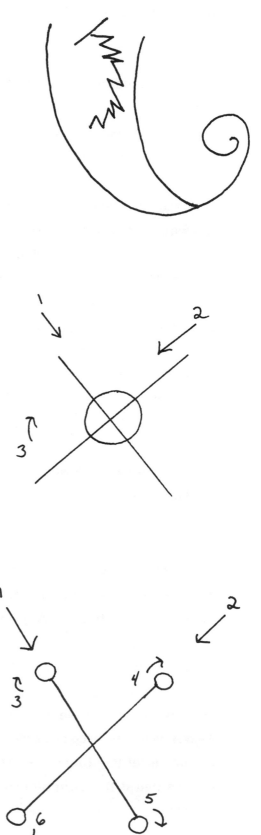

Desires is used to protect and project wants into the future. It represents both clarity of purpose and openness to allow spirit to work through us.

Katherine Szedenik, another of my students, was given three symbols, the first is very much like the one Valerie Weaver was given for Desires. The symbol is turned and it becomes **Peace** and is great for planetary healing. It can be toned "A-OE-A" while drawing. My suggestion would be to work with and meditate on these symbols. In this manner see what works best for you, and what impressions you receive. Symbols get us past the logical left brain and into other realities. Expect the unexpected.

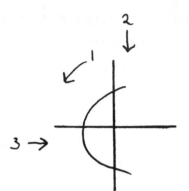

The other two symbols given to Katherine are drawn together. They are **Universal Wisdom & Light**. Katherine loves drawing these symbols on the crown chakra and third eye because it opens these chakras. This symbol can be toned "OMRA" while drawing it.

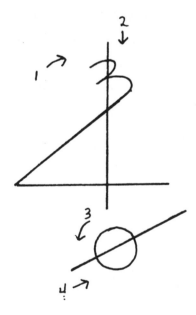

There are two ways in which to draw **Trinity**. To release blockages, cone the fingers of your left hand and draw the triangle three times counterclockwise beginning in the lower left hand corner. Then circle counterclockwise three times. The circling motion can be continued as the blockage is drawn out of the body and up to the Light for transformation. To put energy in, cone the fingers of your right hand and draw the circle clockwise three times; continue drawing the triangle clockwise three times, starting at the top of the triangle. Then lay your hands over the affected area or touch point. Susan Peterson Siegler under guidance has added a five pointed blue star in the center of this triangle which she meditates on. Her guides call it the stillpoint, which is a point of inner balance.

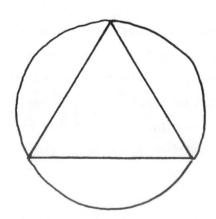

114

Midas Star is a symbol for affluence, not just money. There is a Cree Indian prophecy, "Only after the last tree has been cut down. Only after the last river has been poisoned. Only after the last fish has been caught. Only then will you find that money cannot be eaten." Money is supposed to be an expression of our power and a vehicle for us to be able to do the things we need and want to do. Using numbers from the bible and the Holy Kabbalah Bert Goldman, a Silva instructor, connected them and found Midas Star within the points. Drawing a red line over the bottom horizontal line under the star increases and grounds the energy. I invite you to try it.

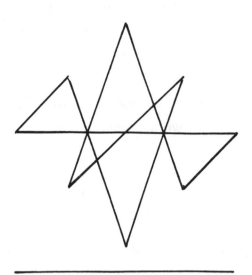

The swirl in this symbol is an energizer; the open "M" represents the feminine power that is present in all women. Men can also benefit from this symbol, as it opens their nurturing, creative, healing nature. To use it, we can pray to the Mother aspect of God for aid in whatever our need is. This symbol like all others can be energized with Cho Ku Rays. Calling upon **Mary**'s name three times as we draw the M, we then send her the symbols, asking her to further empower them and send energy back for healing. Other masters, saints and angels will help us in like manner with other healing symbols if we ask. We can also send healing symbols to them and ask them to send the healing to people who have asked us for healing, or we can ask that the healing be sent to Mother Earth. Or we can draw this symbol or other healing symbols in the sand or earth with our coned fingers.

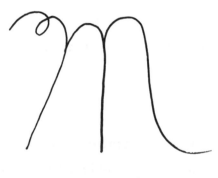

This powerful symbol represents **Christ Light**. It draws the cancer of the spirit and other negative energies into the point where all of the lines converge. It is here that energy is transformed. We draw the long line first, which in this symbol is the focus of power; then the two V's. To use it we focus above our crown. See the Christ Light and

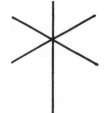

115

the symbol. Visualize the symbol, Light and love coming into us and lighting all of the dark corners and secret closets where hidden skeletons lie. This symbol can be energized with Cho Ku Rays and sent to the Crystalline White Light. Pray for help and then feel the energy returning. Like most symbols, Mary and Christ Light are not initiations symbols. How they work depends entirely upon how much healing energy we personally are able to channel. When I work with these two symbols I usually draw and energize Christ Light first and then Mary. The high vibration is subtle but powerful.

We can get creative in our use of symbols. **Jupiter** is the planet of abundance, manifestation and expansion. There is an astrological sign for Jupiter (Page 127). Jupiter also represents horses. Pegasus, the winged horse, is an archetypal form that found its way into the pages of mythology. The comet that hit Jupiter in July of 1994 is sending waves of Jupiter-type energy back to earth. To tune into and ground the energy of abundance, manifestation and expansion for Earth and for ourselves, we could empower the symbol of Jupiter with Cho Ku Rays (front and back) and then chant, "Pegasus, Jupiter, Pegasus, Jupiter, Pegasus, Jupiter, etc." The intonation is like that of a galloping horse. Watch with your third eye. An alternative symbol combination might be Shanti or Mara, both Cho Ku Rays and Jupiter. It is fun to experiment, and when this is done with an open, loving heart, leaving the details to Mother-Father God, something good is bound to happen.

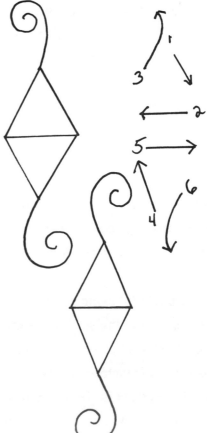

Hosanna was channeled in by Eileen Gurhy of New York City. It is drawn in two continuous lines. Begin in the upper right hand corner and draw down, across, up and spiral. Say, "Hosanna, Hosanna, Hosanna." The second line begins in the lower left hand corner. Draw up, across, down and spiral. Say, "Hosanna, Hosanna, Hosanna." Then punch the triangles in the middle. The first way of drawing Hosanna (with the upper spiral to the left and the lower spiral to the right) radiates clearing energy outwards. The second way of drawing Hosanna focuses in on specific issues. The following is a clearing using Hosanna. The reason why invocations are done three times is to raise our vibration; the vibration of the saints and angels is already raised. First we send Hosanna to St. Michael, then to the angels of the violet fire and then to St. Germane:

116

Draw Cho Ku Rays and Hosanna. "Saint Michael the Archangel. Saint Michael the Archangel. Saint Michael the Archangel take your red flaming sword and cut and release any ties, any cords not of God's Desire between _____ and _____. Cut free, cut free by your red flaming sword any ties, any cords not of God's Desire. Release, release by your red flaming sword any ties, any cords not of God's Desire." Visualize Saint Michael and this process unfolding.

Draw Cho Ku Rays and Hosanna. "Angels of the Violet Fire. Angels of the Violet Fire. Angels of the Violet Fire take any psychic debris that Michael is cutting free with his red flaming sword, any ties, any cords not of God's Desire between _____ and _____. And release, release to the Violet Fire any ties, any cords not of God's Desire. Transform, transform by Violet Fire any ties, any cords not of God's Desire. Transmute, transmute by Violet Fire any ties, any cords not of God's Desire." Visualize!

Draw Cho Ku Rays and Hosanna. "Saint Germane, Saint Germane, Saint Germane, I invoke your sweet name, keeper of the Violet Flame. Take any psychic debris that the Angels of the Violet Fire are bringing to thee that Michael is cutting free by his red flaming sword any ties, any cords not of God's Desire between _____ and _____. And release, release to the Violet Fire any ties, any cords not of God's Desire. Transmute, transmute by Violet Fire any ties, any cords not of God's Desire. Transform, transform by Violet Fire any ties, any cords not of God's Desire." Visualize!

Immediately fill the void: "I call forth the great celestial angels and archangels to fill any voids with colors, tones, symbols, flower remedies, and herbs that are needed for perfect and divine healing. Father-Mother God, please give a very special blessing to those beings who have helped with this clearing and healing, and let their blessing be now, dear Father-Mother God, please let it be now."

Please note that Michael's color is not the traditional blue. Brian Johnson, a Chicago psychologist and one of my students, has been given alternative colors for most of the archangels as well as other archangels of healing by his guide, Rama. Brian is presently writing a book on how Jesus healed through the holy archangels and the Angelic Host entitled, <u>The Jesus Manuscript</u> subtitled, <u>A Look at Healing Rays through the Eyes of an Egyptian</u>. Katherine Ettmayer and I were given the following colors for the commonly known archangels: Michael comes in on a crimson red ray. Uriel (a very feminine presence) is a soft yellow. Gabriel's color is a soft pink (again a feminine presence). Raphael is various shades of green. This is <u>not</u> to say that each archangel only works with one color.

In the blank lines on the clearing the healer can place the names of 2 people who are bound unhealthfully to one another. There should only be love between us. For example, "between Mary and John." You can also use this for planetary healing, in this case saying, "between earth and the forces that would hold her back." Another possible symbol combination for clearings might be to draw both Hosanna symbols with Cho Ku Rays in between.

In hands-on healing I can draw symbols on my clients only <u>after</u> I ask for their permission. After drawing the symbols over the body, I place my hands on the area. If I am psychically tuned in to my spirit guides, angels and my client, I can direct the symbols to go wherever they are needed. As long as we leave everything in divine order, and realize that the symbols and healing come from Mother-Father God, we cannot go wrong!

In **absentee healing** I can send <u>any symbol</u> to anyone. I do not have to call and ask for their permission first because I am not violating their free will choice. They are at liberty to either accept or reject the healing energy. If they do reject the energy; however, I cannot send the symbols again unless they either ask for absentee healing or if I am impressed to send them again after there has been a <u>noticeable</u> character change. There have also been occasions when I have arranged a time in advance with a client where they are meditating and I am visualizing and sending symbols. Some people make a list of individuals who need healing and send symbols to the list. We can even draw healing symbols on the local telephone book and ask that healing be sent to those who are open to receiving the energy. There are lots of possibilities!

In sending symbols several things are happening. By concentrating on the symbol, I am holding the consciousness of that symbol. Since we are both individuals and also a part of the Oneness of All There Is, in a very real sense the person to whom I am sending healing and healing symbols to is present with me. Time and space do not exist the way we understand it on this three-dimensional plane.

Books on spirituality will talk about our left side being our receiving side, while the right side is our sending side. With the Reiki energy I can send energy with either or both hands. I can pull off misqualified energy with either or both hands. However, the left side remains more effective in drawing or receiving; the right side is more powerful in sending. Healing can be sent over the telephone wire with or without the symbols. The healer holds onto the telephone cord with their right hand; the healee holds onto the cord with their left hand.

When I send healing symbols, I close my eyes either while I am drawing or right after I have drawn the symbols. I usually draw the symbols in the air in front of me, but I can also draw them in the palms of my hands *(which can also be done in hands-on-healing with the client's permission)*. Immediately after drawing them I use my inner vision to see what is happening. I can hold the palms of my hands out and visualize the energy going to the healee. I can turn the palms of my hands so that they are facing one another and visualize the individual between my hands. If I know where the symptoms are, I can place my hands on my own body either on the appropriate touch point(s) or on the involved area while visualizing the individual. Many Reiki classes teach the student to visualize the thigh of their leg as being the individual lying down with one leg being the front, the other the back. All of these methods and others work.

While I am using my second sight I can use the same healing techniques in absentee healing that I use in hands-on-healing. I can use my physical hands to pull or lift off misqualified energy, drain and then fill the voids with Light and color. Or I may simply watch spirit helpers and angels work. Sometimes I see the individual, other times the symbol, or I feel what's happening.

If I am working with a group of healers, or if I am teaching a second degree Reiki class we sit in a circle. We can send energy to world events, situations, places, or even to one another, but I like to begin with people that we know so that information received during the healing can be verified. Each person takes a turn speaking the first name only of an individual who comes to mind. We then all draw the same healing symbols, saying the name of each symbol 3 times, and then say, "To _____ (first name of individual)." After the healing each person in the circle shares what s/he saw, heard or felt. In this way the individual who placed the name in the circle can provide confirmation or clarification because they know the healee. I have found this to be a very good way to teach individuals to do psychic readings in healing. Sometimes everyone in the circle is working on a different issue on the same individual; sometimes several healers are working on the same issue, but receive different visual metaphors.

In these group situations sometimes the angels will give me the same metaphor for everyone we send healing to, but it is like a theme in variation. Once I saw everyone we sent healing to as a dog, not a person. The type of dog that I saw them as related to their personality; and the injury or disease I saw in the dog's body paralleled the body part that the healee had issues with. Even the ages correlated; I saw young children as puppies and elderly people as dogs with traces of gray hair. One time in New York my angelic theme for the evening was flowers. We were sending healing to one of Sean Grealy's friends in Ireland when I saw a carpet of flowers. Frustrated I asked Straight Arrow, "Now what does this mean?" Immediately the blanket of

119

flowers fell to the ground revealing a coffin. The woman next to me saw the same outcome with her second sight but different metaphors. She saw an empty hospital bed. The sheets were fresh and there was a clean nightshirt lying on top of the bed. The lights were turned down. Sean's friend died two weeks later. Perhaps the Reiki energy helped him in his transition, which will happen if the body is too far gone or if it is their time to transcend.

Robert Wachsberger of California found that if we put a glass of water in the center of the circle, we could all send energy to the water. The healer who put the individual's name into the circle concentrates on the individual. Then that same healer drinks the water, and if the individual is open, s/he will receive the healing.

Crystals come from the earth and hold the same electromagnetic energy that is found in the earth. They can be programmed with healing symbols and healing. What we often forget to do is lock in the program, and give the instructions that we are the only ones who can change or alter the programing. We can then use these crystal for hands-on or distant healing work. We can use crystals in distant or in hands-on-healing. When we are finished using them, crystal should be cleared. If we do not clear our crystals, or if someone tries to misuse them, the crystals can become cloudy and eventually loose all of their vital force energy. Crystals can also shut down if they fall into the wrong hands.

Within the healing circle we can set up a circle of Light. This can be done in any number of ways. We can hold hands and visualize and feel the energy running through our hands (typically in through our crowns, out the right hand and into the left hand of the person sitting next to us). Then we fill the circle with Light. We can send symbols into the center and then invite any earth-bound spirit who wishes to make their transition into the Light to take the hand of an angel and walk into the center. Oftentimes there is a crowd waiting. Also within this circle we can visualize places on earth, or Mother Earth and the moon as well. We send energy, pull off negativity and fill the voids with Light and color. The potentials are inexhaustible.

After the Rune masters drew their symbols, they would extend their left arm upwards, wrist and elbow unbent. Right arm would be held down at the side, but with the right palm parallel to the earth. In this manner they would draw their creation in with their left hand and arm, and ground it or make it earth form with the right. This is also the way the magician stands in the Tarot. This is also the way Hitler stood, drawing in the energy of the crowd for his own purposes. The Nazis didn't just have an inner circle of individuals who misused psychic energy, they all did, and very specifically the symbols from the Runes. While they lived high on the hog for a long time, when the end came, it came crashing down upon them. Just because a group abuses a Universal system doesn't mean that we cannot clear the symbols and use them correctly. Thus, the symbols from the Runes can safely be energized with Cho Ku Rays.

This ability to draw in Universal energy can be done with or without drawing symbols, which is one reason why people who study Tai Chi and other martial arts take Reiki. Let me use a practical example, one that can be used in self-healing for a pain anywhere on the body. I can do this with or without drawing the healing symbols first. I stretch my left arm upwards, wrist and elbow unbent, and pull in life force energy into my left hand. At the same time I hold a washcloth in my right hand. The cloth can be dry, or rinsed in hot or cold water beforehand; and for large areas or those difficult to reach, a scarf can be used. Then I pass my left hand over the washcloth several times (I like to do things in multiples of 3's). I can repeat the process a couple of more times, and then I place the cloth on the pain. This process can also be used with herbs, for example, if the pain is in my sinuses, I may want to boil some water and then steep Echinacea in the water. Allowing the water to cool to touch, I then soak the washcloth in the water prior to pulling in the Chi. *(This same method can be used to charge amulets or crystals with Universal energy.)*

I can also use the archetypal universal symbols from Egypt for healing. Cartouche is the oval within which the hieroglyphs are drawn. The Way of Cartouche by Murry Hope does an excellent job of explaining 25 fundamental symbols. These symbols survived Atlantis. Most people are very familiar with some of these symbols. The Caduceus, the winged staff with 2 intertwining snakes, is the symbol adopted by the American Medical Association. In Egyptian lore it is the symbol of Thoth, patron of healers. Many of the early ascended masters found their way into mythology by ancient storytellers, much the way we tell our children the tales of the saints. Pyramid is found on the back of the U. S. dollar bill, and is a powerful symbol for grounding and healing. The Mayan high priests used to sit in lotus position (which is the human body imitating the pyramid) on top of the pyramids. They would then visualize the sun's energy coming into their crowns, going down through the pyramid, and out onto the land for the benefit of all the people. Mankind tends to see royalty as fearful powers we are to be subservient to. Rather, those who would be king, high priestess, etc. serve the people and their authority comes through respect because they are aligned with, not demolishing the forces of nature.

The initiation into Egyptian symbols brings about a state of heightened awareness. In Egypt symbols were respected as higher principles. Symbols had designated values and were worked with for thousands and thousands of years in Egypt and prior to that in Atlantis. If perchance the symbols initially didn't hold consciousness, by intention and repeated use they began to, and they retain that energy today. Psychics who are initiated into the Egyptian symbols receive more and clearer information, whether they read tarot cards or do astrology readings. Universal concepts remain the same regardless if the shape of the symbol is a Rune, Egyptian hieroglyph, or astrological sign. I initiated Aaron Sapiro into the Egyptian symbols and taught him how to do the Egyptian initiations. Here's what Aaron had to say, *"I woke up at 4:00 am with an absolutely clear understanding of the 24 Runes and of the order in which they usually appear in the arrangement called the Elder Futhark. What this means to me is that I can now read them syntactically, in whatever order they occur. Apparently the Cartouche initiation worked!"* He used the same initiation procedure and initiated his wife using the symbols from the Runes. It worked and the *"next day she could understand the complex relationships among the Tarot cards as well as the connection between the Tarot and the Kabbalah."*

I asked Cocorah, who had gone through these Egyptian initiations and was channeling a spirit guide, Jake, what the effects of the initiation were. Jake answered that he could see more clearly and that he was able to bring in through Cocorah clearer, more in depth information. When I am working on a client during a healing session, the Egyptian initiations help me in facilitating the healing process by providing information concerning my client. This information also comes in the form of a definite awareness within my own body. I feel where the blockages are, and I can feel energy when the blocks start moving. This awareness is not at all painful, and works in combination with my inner knowing. It can be an odd sensation to suddenly feel my spleen. When I feel glands or organs within me, I am less in my head and have a much more three-dimensional sensation of my form.

In meditation and dreams people are sometimes given personal symbols to use. Before using any new symbol it is wise to check out who gave us the symbol, if they came in the Love of Christ, and if the symbols themselves are clear. We all have the tools to check and clear with. If we are using a symbol that is cleared and negativity is brought up from within us, I have found that it is best to breath into the emotion or thought form, search within myself for the source of the conflict, and continue working with the symbol until the negative pattern is worked out.

There are some symbols that anyone can use. There are others that one has to be initiated into before they can be used. Depending on the level of healing energy that you have been born with, gathered, or been initiated into depends on how effectively the symbols will work. If you are in the aura of a teacher who is sending symbols and you are open, you can tune in and send symbols along with the teacher. It is a good way to try out the energy and see if it is for you.

Feng Shui and the Elemental Forces

Tao is God in action; Taoism is a way of living life in harmony with God and nature. Native American mysticism held an awareness that everything is part of a divine plan. They expressed this in ceremony and in the act of conscious living. Mayans worked through this same concept with their calendars, and incorporated these teachings into their daily lives. Three different expressions of spiritualism, three different names for God. All three honored nature and the cosmos as a manifestation of God.

The Taoist philosophy began in China twenty-five-hundred year's ago when Lao Tzu, a gifted philosopher and scholar, wrote Tao Te Ching. Taoism covers all aspects of ones life on earth, with different disciplines found within the philosophy. For example, Chi Kung Masters moved energy through the human body to chase out the evil winds (blockages) and bring in healthy Chi (energy). Feng Shui Masters work with the same elemental universal energy, but they moved it within the living environment for the purpose of facilitating change. Thus, the same energy used for healing can also be used in the home and place of business.

The Chinese use five elements rather than four, but because Feng Shui operates on universal principles, it does work. For example, in western astrology my sun sign is Pisces and my moon and ascendant are both Capricorn; in eastern or Jyotish astrology I am an Aquarian with a Sagittarian moon and ascendant. Because both systems are founded in Universal concepts I am told basically the same things about myself in either reading. However, when I am looking at one system, be it eastern or western, I have to remain in that system. It doesn't work to mix apples and oranges. For example, a friend of mine purchased Horoscopes of the Western Hemisphere by Mark Penfield so that she could compare her birth chart with the birth charts of the states and cities in order to find the ideal place for her to live. We are all supposed to be the star of our own life. Initially she compared her eastern Jyotish chart to all of the state and city western charts; when she discovered her error, she had to go back and use her western chart. *(As a side note, in using this book, the deciding factor is to compare your birth chart, as if you had been born in that city , with the astrological charts for the city and state.)*

Shamanism, magic, homeopathy and Feng Shui survived the test of time because they work and are practical. Chi Kung Masters and Feng Shui Masters were paid well. The energy they channeled and the knowledge they possessed brought about profound changes. Good Feng Shui Masters could literally tip the scales of fortune. Many people have experienced physical healings with Universal energy. Can you imagine what would happen if this same energy were applied to an environment?

Feng Shui has been referred to as the Chinese art of placement. There are many different sects of Feng Shui, but two fundamental schools - compass and location. Both schools work around a schematic frame, or Ba-Gua, within which the quality of different energies exist. The eight areas of life within the Ba-Gua that can be altered or enhanced are: Career, knowledge and self-cultivation, health and family, money and power, fame and reputation, marriage and partnership, children and inspiration, and travel and helpful people. The compass school is based on a land typography that is particular to China and the Ba-Gua rotates every year. Location determines energy patterns in the placement school, which is the original system. Also, since the Ba-Gua does not change yearly, the location school is far easier to understand.

First and foremost, no matter which school of Feng Shui you are using, there is always an underlying respect for nature. The Chinese would never think of coming into an area and bulldozing it, which alters the energy as well as the beauty of the land. Rather the home or office is set in harmony with the land and co-exists comfortably with nature.

There is a wonderful book out by Sarah Rossbach, <u>Interior Design with Feng Shui</u>, based on a sect within the location school.   There are easy things that anyone can do to initiate change by implementing cures for that which is out of balance.   In simple acts we make statements to Mother-Father God that we are ready for improvements in our lives, and God listens. I do have a few suggestions, many people after reading the book or taking a Feng Shui class activate their Money Corner and their Marriage and Partnership Corner only. Without helpful people nothing is going to happen. Actually all eight areas of ones life should be activated and balanced. My primary intent in this particular chapter is not to replicate a perfectly good book, but rather to address the elemental forces within the location school of Feng Shui.

The first thing you need to do is to find your architectural front doorway, and it does not matter whether or not it is used. It might be easier to stand outside of the house, building or office and then apply what I am about to explain to the interior. If you live in an apartment, your architectural front doorway is not the entrance to the building, but rather your own front door. Within the middle of this front <u>wall</u> *(and it doesn't matter if the doorway is far to the right or left, or in the middle)* is the element **water**.   Facing the front of your home or office from the outside, in the middle of the wall to your left is the element **wood**.   In the middle of the back wall is the element **fire.**   In the center of the building is the element **earth**. And in the middle

124

of the right hand wall, as you are facing the front of your home from the outside, is the element **metal**. The <u>positive cycle of the 5 elements is</u>: Wood produces fire, fire produces earth, earth produces metal, metal produces water, water produces wood.

The <u>destructive cycle of the 5 elements is</u>: Metal destroys wood, wood destroys (absorbs) earth, earth destroys (absorbs) water, water destroys fire, fire destroys metal.   Thus, whenever you find an element that destroys another element in that element's particular area, there will be problems. The cure or solution is to supply the missing element. We will go through these one by one so that you have a clear understanding of the concept.

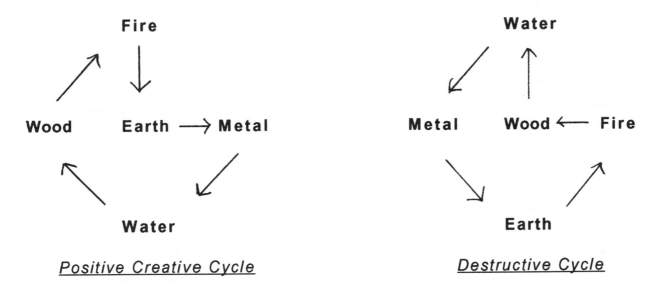

<u>*Positive Creative Cycle*</u>   <u>*Destructive Cycle*</u>

The most frequently occurring problem that I find is water along the back wall, be it a sink, tub, toilet, pool *(and if there is an outdoor pool close to the back wall of the house, it can cause problems)*, etc. The fame and reputation area of the Ba-Gua is along the back wall of the house. <u>Water puts out fire</u>, it can also put out the fires of fame or throw water on your reputation. This particular problem can also adversely affect the eyes. The cure is not to get a plumber and move the fixtures or fill in the pool with cement, but rather to supply the missing element. Between water and fire is wood, so the cure is to put up something green or wooden over the sink, or whatever fixture is running or holding water. (In addition a bowl of rice should be place on the back of a toilet, which can be disguised by placing potpourri over it.)

Let us say that a home has a courtyard in the center of the house in which trees are planted. <u>Wood destroys earth</u>. Between earth and wood is the element fire. Fire is missing. As a barbecue grill might be inappropriate or even dangerous, the color red will serve the purpose.

If there is metal on or within the wall to the left, which is where wood abides, the <u>metal will destroy wood.</u> Corresponding physical problems can be with the feet. As this is the health and family wall, there could be other health issues or family disruption. The missing element is water, as it lies between metal and wood. The cure is the element water, such as a fish tank. A photograph, painting or drawing of water will also work if that picture conveys strongly the energy of water. The alternative cure is the color black.

<u>Earth destroys water</u>. If there are potted plants along the front wall, or if the front wall is stone, it can be harmful to your career and may affect your ears. Between earth and water is metal. Either the missing element metal or the color white along the front wall is required for the cure.

If the kitchen stove or fireplace is against the wall to the right, you may have mouth problems. <u>Fire destroys metal</u>, and it can also adversely affect your children or your inspiration, as this is where these two qualities lie. The missing element is earth, as it lies between fire and metal. Rocks, plants or the color yellow will provide the cure.

Each of the elemental forces is directly related to one of the 5 planets: Wood with Jupiter. Fire with Mars. Earth with Saturn. Metal with Venus. Water with Mercury. Both mountains and buildings by their shapes exhibit characteristics of the elements and their corresponding planets. Whenever you have natural or man-made shapes that are next to one another and exhibit the qualities of 2 elements that are in a destructive phase, the missing element needs to be added.

<u>Fire and Mars</u>: Bold mountains with straight peaks running out to a sharp point. Tall, pointed

buildings. Best businesses in these types of structures are those dealing with energy.

<u>Earth and Saturn</u>: Mountains with extensive plateaus. Older, heavy buildings, especially those

built of stone, marble and other earth materials. Big colonial homes and structures with flat roofs. Most businesses do well in these kinds of buildings.

<u>Metal and Venus</u>: Mountains with softly rounded peaks. Venus-type buildings are churches with crosses and softly rounded domes. Buildings that are rich and ornate. Best business is big business and banks.

<u>Water and Mercury</u>: Mountains with a cupola shaped top. Buildings with scalloped or

 projecting roofs. Businesses that tend to thrive in these structures are schools, libraries, transportation and communication.

<u>Wood and Jupiter</u>: Bold mountains with straight peaks whose top is broken off (flat and narrow). Jupiter-type buildings are tall and straight with a flat top. Best businesses in these buildings are schools, bookstores and those dealing with philosophy.

Again we look to the destructive cycle. <u>Metal destroys wood.</u> If two buildings are next to one another and one is characteristically metal-Venus and the other wood-Jupiter, the missing element is water. A water fountain or the color black between the buildings is needed for the cure.

<u>Wood destroys earth</u>. If one building is wood-Jupiter and the other earth-Saturn in construction, the missing element is fire. Torches may not be possible, the color red is certainly probable.

<u>Earth destroys water</u>. If one adjacent building is earth-Saturn and the other is water-Mercury, the missing element is metal. A bronze statue, or the color white will provide the cure.

<u>Water destroys fire</u>. One building is a water-Mercury type, the other a fire-Mars type. The missing element is wood and the cure is something green and wooden, like planting trees. Very effective and easy to do, and also brings in positively the forces of nature.

<u>Fire destroys metal</u>. A fire-Mars building is next to a metal-Venus building. The missing element is earth. Plant a flower garden behind a rock wall, a large rock display or the color yellow provides the cure.

Generally speaking, any lines (roads or waterways) that run off in straight lines, are steep or are sharply angled create dangerous energy. It is especially dangerous when the line points towards the building. When Chi runs too fast, it becomes Sha (long hallways or a series of 3 or more doors have the same effect inside a building). Outdoors the cure typically is trees in the backyard and a water fountain in the front. Indoors a multifaceted crystal is hung in the middle of the hallway. Depending upon the length of the hallway, more than one crystal may be required. Gentle, graceful curves, natural settings and elevations are the best locations.

Beautifying and bringing nature back into cities would result in an advantageous boom to business. Productive cities like New York are often famous for their beautiful parks.

The Chinese also worked with ley (light) lines which they called the dragon and the tiger. In using both natural structures and constructing holy places and shrines, they venerated and utilized the forces of nature. In both Celtic and Chinese traditions the burial of the dead in relationship to these energy lines was an important way for the ancestors to benefit the living.

In Feng Shui working with the elemental forces, the spirit of the land and the ancestors who walked the land before us brings about good karma and beneficial results. It was also the job of the Feng Shui Master to release harmful energies. Those energies that we call underlings or earth-bound souls can be released to the Light through clearings and prayers. Smudging with sage and cedar can also help. Sometimes I need to go to every window and door with a burning white candle and holy water. Making the sign of the cross I say the complete "Our Father".

It is also important to look for the thought forms behind objects within and around the home or office. For example, a mask of Medusa in the Marriage and Partnership Corner may well serve the purpose of keeping likely suitors away even though it may have all the right colors; pink, red and white. One of my clients in Chicago had a painting of red, black and green in his Money Corner. However, it was a painting of a hobo. Even though he was a doctor, he was headed for bankruptcy. The picture of the hobo was thrown out! On the other hand, I have found that lucky objects can be those other than typically considered to be Feng Shui activators. A lot depends upon the energy within a talisman, painting, crystal, etc. and upon the spiritual preference of the individual living in the house. Another woman in Chicago had a missing corner, which also means a missing aspect to ones life. However, when I dowsed, it was not missing. She had a painting of a Native American on the wall that was pulling in the missing aspect. She did not need a mirror.

Some people have a conception, or rather a misconception, that there is only room at the top for just so many individuals and they want to be counted in as one of them. From my own career perspective, as an educator, I view that my job as a teacher is to teach myself out of a job. I release what I know for the benefit of others, and do not hold back so that I create the illusion of being ahead of everyone else. When I am empty, Mother-Father God refills me with more than my measure of giving. To go on we all need to let go of our fear that Yahweh will not provide. We can all utilize Feng Shui and the elemental forces for our advancement and the creation of a golden age. Allah is indeed good.

128

Ceremonies and Magic

Why do I teach people how to do magic? Because for the most part the wrong people already know how to do it and are using it for purposes of serving their will! Hitler had perfect past-life recall of being one of the leaders of the Holy Inquisition. In that same lifetime he was also an adept black magician. Trevors Ravenscroft describes this in detail in The Spear of Destiny.

We call magic that is manipulative black magic. Why? The definition of the color black is that which is hidden and unseen. The definition of the color white is that which is known and seen. If an individual knew that a magician wanted to control them or manipulate something from them, the magic would either not work or not be as effective. A magician wishing to misuse psychic powers works exclusively with a black ray. Without the balance of white, the black is no longer the velvet black of the void, the womb of the Goddess; rather it becomes a dull, dense color. The other extreme would be like standing under a 10,000 watt light bulb, where everything is held accountable and under close scrutiny, like far right-wing (Hitler) and far left-wing (Stalin) politics. Often black magicians hold others suspect and seek control of even the most trivial of actions; thus, in the extremes are found similarities. In The Spear of Destiny, which inspired the movie Indiana Jones, Trevors Ravenscroft documents how the Nazis practiced black magic, and not just a mere handful of officers in the inner circle. Using black magic to control others, to live in the illusion that one is above the laws of man and God, can last for only a short period of time. When God says, "Enough!" the ending is sudden, dramatic and painful to say the least.

Let's begin by dispelling black magic. Black magicians work with what we would call the forces of evil; the Illuminati think they are working with an evil god. It is not the physical act of turning an object up-side-down or drawing a symbol backwards that creates evil. If I draw a counterclockwise circle, it will look clockwise to you. It is not the perspective, but rather it is the intent that creates black magic. These magicians use destructive, negative emotions that they may build up for a week or even more. They repeat spells that utilize some of the foulest things you would probably never in your wildest imagination think of. While they stand in the middle of a pentagram for protection, they call up demons and underlings to carry out their Luciferian pacts.

How do I know these things? I read them in a book. Yes, there are some magic books out that are divided into sections of white and black magic, and I would like to add that some of the spells listed under white magic are extremely manipulative. Perhaps they are listed there because their ingredients are not as foul as those listed under black magic? This is neither recommended reading, nor is it for the faint of heart. You may find if difficult to stay out of judgement. I know that I did.

Why did I read this book? Because my son, Lee, gave it to me for my birthday, and he and I have a past life connection and an ability to help one another. When he was young he had terrible nightmares and would frequently come into my bedroom at night for reassurance. One night as I lay in bed poised between consciousness and sleep I heard a man's voice come out of my nine-year-old son's bedroom loudly exclaiming, "Oh, Shit!" I immediately got up. When I reached Lee, he was crying. I asked him to tell me his dream. Lee said that he had been on a submarine that had been hit by a torpedo and he had blown up. I tuned in and told him that he had recalled another lifetime, and that the angels were now busy making him whole again. He fell back asleep and he never had those nightmares again.

After reading the book I knew how to break black magic spells. How does one do this? In three ways: The first is by sending love and compassion to the magician. They neither comprehend nor can they handle unconditional love. If the magician has used someone else as the vehicle through which the spell was sent, unconditional love I send back will go through this individual to the source. Secondly, the Egyptian mirror of Hathor, or visualizing a mirror in my aura, or asking the angels to place mirrors around me repels black magic. In whatever way I wish to set the mirrors, as long as I place them with unconditional love, negative thought forms will be transformed in love and sent back to the magician. The magician then has the free-will choice to accept or reject his/her karma. If the karma is rejected it comes back to me. However, if I transform the black magic in love before I send it back, then the declined karma will be transmuted again, and comes back to me, not as a curse, but as blessings and gifts. Thirdly, I can use the Hosanna clearing on the spell, my client, and I can even send the clearing back to the magician. To keep black magic from returning I ask, "What am I doing to allow this "negative" energy in?" This is not easy! Healing our own issues insures that black magic, no matter how powerful, will never touch us.

As more Light comes to this planet on a daily basis many of the demons that black magicians have worked with in the past are either making their own transition into the Light or leaving the planet. Also many of Earth's dark, heavy places are being transformed and healed. For some people who do planetary healing, it looks and feels like encrusted layers are coming off Earth one level at a time. Behind each layer is a thick ooze that has to be drained and filled with Light. When this has been healed, another level comes up for healing, transformation and release. In this manner black magicians are losing their power base, and because they have abused the energy, their own psychic abilities as well.

The Light is able to bring deceptions up to the surface. Light is able to do this because lies, unlike the truth, have no weight or substance to them. One has to keep telling more lies to keep the original lie down. A fabricated story becomes elaborate; the Truth is always simple. A good example of this is the assassination of John F. Kennedy. It won't go away!

Black magicians have been using or rather misusing some powerful symbols and then turning around and telling us that they are "evil" so that we won't use them. In magic, the circumference of the circle of the pentagram represents what the Hindus call Brahman, what we refer to as Absolute Consciousness. Contained within the circle is a five-pointed star, the star of the ancients. The five points represent the four elements and spirit. It is a tool for manifestation. The ram is not the symbol of the devil. The devil has neither regard for, nor wishes to emulate nature. Nature is a manifestation of God, Whom the devil holds in contempt.

<u>To dispel and manifest</u> (principle of creativity originating from womb of Mother-God): Have clear intention. Coning the fingers of both hands, draw a five-pointed star backwards, then a clockwise circle beginning at the top, and punch it in the middle. Next draw a counterclockwise circle beginning at the bottom, then a five-pointed star, and punch it in the middle.

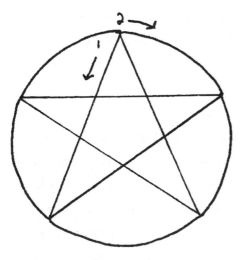

Banishing or Clearing

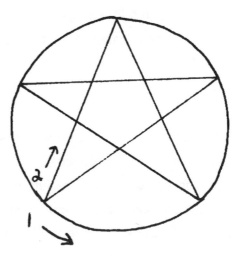

Drawing or Creative

Kay Gloege's spirit guides told her Ram is "striking force." It is the energy which sends the magic off. Black is the color of the Great Void, Great Mystery. Raven is magic; crow is shape shifting. The half man/half goat figure again, is not the devil, but Pan. Pan is neither a drunkard nor a rapist, he is symbolic of our connectedness to nature. Stories are told of Atlantian scientists who abused animals and conducted unnatural experiments. They created beings that were half man and half beast, so to speak. Through a fatal flaw they eventually died off, but while they lived they were subjected to humiliation and abuse. Many souls, including those reincarnated souls of the scientists who were responsible, evolved and worked through their karma in these forms. Chiron, half man/half horse, is the wounded healer.

I was raised in the Roman Catholic religion. There always have been nuns, priests and other church officials who compassionately worked for humanity. And not all popes were privy to the original doctrines of Jesus. Among the things that I did learn from the Church was the fact that the personalities of the saints survived death; we could pray to them. The old Latin Mass had a real sense of ceremonial ritual. And each year began another predictable liturgical calendar, honoring specific times and events.

All mysticisms honoring Goddess, the Mother aspect of God, performed simple ceremonies using the simple things of earth. Eye of Knut and other horrific sounding ingredients were code names for herbs the wise women used. In this way the witches bravely protected the knowledge so that their torturers would not obtain and abuse these herbs in black magic ceremonies. White magic utilizes the power of the four directions, the four elemental forces and is particularly effective when done in conjunction with lunar phases. The moon represents the feminine. There are 13 moon cycles in a solar year; 13 is an auspicious number, not an evil or unlucky one. For us to be using a Roman 12 month calendar is like putting a western saddle on a horse. "What happened? Where's the horse?" By using the Gregorian calendar we emphasize the division between God and Goddess, and we are out of synchronicity with nature.

In utilizing the power of the moon, expansive magic, such as the accumulation of wealth for an intended purpose, is best begun under the new moon, allowing the power of the growing, waxing moon to work for us. While the full moon is a time for fulfillment, magic that is decreasing in nature, such as loosing a bad habit, disease or extra pounds, is best begun under the full moon. Thus, allowing the waning moon to assist us in diminishing the unwanted trait or energy. Utilizing the power of seasonal changes, and planetary aspects that are occurring at the time further increases the might and results of white magic.

As with shamanic work, it is vital to have clear intentions and leave the details to Divine Order. Purposes for performing white magic can be for getting new guides, healing, resources, or psychically obtained information or divination. Please notice that the root word of divination is divine. Divination is knowledge obtained from divine sources.

An altar is often created in the center of the circle. In this manner we both pull in and honor the four directions and four elements. One way to do this is to find a red cloth *(red to ground and aid the physical manifestation).* Different native tribes, different mystical cults have different placements for the four elemental forces. This is the placement that I use that works for me: East wind brings spiritual illumination, transformation, creativity and passion, here we find the element fire. Place a candle in the east. White is the most popular; however, you can adjust the color to your need. To dress a candle with oil *(again the oil can be significant of your want)* begin in the middle and go up to the wick, go back to the middle and apply the oil downwards. Symbols can also be etched into the candle specific of your desires. When you are ready to light the candle, make a full arch with your arm, name the candle as you light it *(again the name you assign the candle can be appropriate to the magic you are performing).* It works in this manner. If I want to create abundance I would anoint a green candle with frankincense, draw the symbols Cho Ku Rays and Shanti or Mara on it and then place it in the east. As I light the candle I would say something like, "I name you Jupiter and I call upon the holy ones to assist me." I would do this on or within three days <u>after</u> the dark moon. The three days prior to the dark moon is a good time to complete projects, not begin them! If the planet Jupiter is also making some nice aspects in the heavens, the magic will increase, as Jupiter is an energy of expansion, manifestation and wealth. Matches as well as candles should never be blown out, you loose about 40% of the energy.

Porcupine sits in the south of the medicine wheel. Here is the place of emotions and water. Within water the qualities of love, healing, devotion and psychic development are found. Place a dish of water, spring water or ocean water if you can, in the south. My cats, Ziggy and Janis, prefer this water to the water in their drinking bowl. White magic is easy, I just keep refilling the dish.

The west of the medicine wheel is the place of earth. The attributes of earth are grounding and foundation, prosperity, introspection and prayer. Bear sits in the west. Deep winter hibernation suggests the skill of introspection. Introspection and meditation help us from becoming entrapped in the physical trance state. Prosperity is a viable tool for us to use, not an end in itself. Place a stone, crystal or both in the west. Some people place a vessel of earth here.

North wind brings the element of air. Characteristics of air are wisdom and knowledge, communication (telepathic included), and gratitude. Together the four elements comprise all of the things we need. Place either a knife (preferable one with a white handle) in the north. As feathers cut through air, a feather will work as well.

When the altar is set and with clear intentions in mind, I need to call in spirit helpers, angels, personal spirit guides, ancestors (those who have walked before me), the 4 elements and 4 directions. I then call upon the Goddess to come from the earth and into our hearts, and for God to come from the heavens and into our hearts. In this way we become a part of the Whole and our hearts become the center of the medicine wheel or circle of life. From the center we pull in the energies and qualities of the 4 directions and 4 elements so that Mother-Father God's Love and the talents we have been blessed with can flow through us.

I perform new and full moon ceremonies with the people I am with wherever I happen to be on planet earth. The direction of focus always remains the same for the elemental forces; however, the quality of the winds change. In the Midwest of the United States I use the following traits: East Wind is dazzling and fresh. South Wind is hot and fiery. West Wind is bountiful and buoyant. North Wind is cold and mighty. For example, these same wind qualities are not going to work in the southern hemisphere. I call all the energies in verbally, with a drum or a combination of both.   Michael Drake has an audio tape with some wonderful drumming patterns specifically designed and intended to invoke the 4 elements, which are also in the directions I described.

In performing magic the amount of personal energy held by the priest, priestess or shaman will determine the impact of the magic. As elemental healing energy is utilized in Feng Shui, so too it is used in magic. People who hold ceremony use universal elemental energy to hold a space for spiritual helpers they honor and call in. The more energy channeled, the more powerful the spirit helpers, and the more the spirit guides and angels will be able to do. During the rituals they work on everyone present, and it is these holy spirits who carry out the magic.

There are many books out on ceremonies that can be used. My personal preference is for those that deal with white magic only. For this reason I use Scott Cunningham's books. The Enchanted Tarot by Amy Zerner and Monte Farber is also a nice place to begin. While there are few guarantees in this world, the magic of the Wheel of Fortune card works every time for me. We find out by doing magic which enchantments or spells work best. Incantations that rhyme are particularly effective. I like knot magic; it is so powerful that it was baned in Europe in the dark ages.

As I mentioned previously, at every new moon and every full moon, no matter where I am in the world, I invite people to come and participate in ceremonies designed to honor and heal earth. I combine holy ceremonial rituals from many sources to bring about beneficial results for all present. Often times those present will receive a signal that something is happening. One thing that always occurs whenever I burn pieces of paper and herbs during a ceremony is that the smoke will reach a certain height, usually about 3 feet off the floor and it will disappear. The smoke is literally carrying petitions and prayers into another dimension. Magic works!

On the way to the barn the day I had the vet put Abez down, I was clearly given the message 3 times that after he died I was to cut and weave some of the hair from his tail. I did this. In California a week later after Dolores did the reading for me on Abez, we went outside so that she could cut my hair. Abez told her, "Now it's your turn, Kathleen." I trust Abez, so I thought, "What is he up to?" After Dolores had been cutting for awhile she said, "I don't know where your hair is going? By all rights the ground around us should be filled with it." Sometimes the wind moves the air in tiny whirlwinds. We both watched one off to the side of us. It was easy to see the bits of my hair shining in the sun in the turning wind. However, about 3 feet above the sidewalk my hair was disappearing into another dimension. It was like watching an etheric vacuum cleaner.

Abez told Dolores that he wanted something of me where he was, and that my hair reminded him of the rainbows that he loved so dearly. Just before he died I had asked Jesus to make Abez a Cahokia Master. I am going through a process; I cannot initiate someone into healing energy that I am not channeling. Dolores tuned in, yes, Jesus had fulfilled my last request, which was also Abez's. Abez was performing magic in front of our eyes.

In ending the ceremony it is important to thank and dismiss the elementals and other spirits so that they can go about and do the work asked of them. I do this by saying something that goes like this, "We thank you blessed, beautiful ones of the Christ. Please take the energy created here to carry out the magic. We invite you also to use the energy for your own evolvement, for those of your own kind, and to aid you in your own work. Dear Father-Mother God please give these wondrous beings a very special blessing and let it be now dear Father-Mother God, please let it be now!" Dr. Valerie Weaver was given the message that when we forget to give thanks and gratitude we slip away from Source and into the illusion of 3-dimensional reality. It is here

135

that our egos become filled with ourselves and not God. It is in this 3-D illusion that we work outside of the Oneness of All There Is.

If possible, I let any candles lit during the ceremony burn out. They can burn out safely in the bathtub or sink in a container of water. If this is not possible, candles are snuffed out. After doing magic, like a psychic reading, it is best to let the energy go and allow it to do its own thing. If I talk about it, I take away from the energy of manifestation, and it takes a grosser physical form or does not physically manifest at all.

Besides performing ceremony, witches also did shamanic journey work. In this state, like Edgar Casey, they would search for answers for their clients and do healing work. While Native American shaman travel through openings into the earth, the witch would lie on the hearth next to the fire, which kept her warm, and spiritually she would travel up the chimney. The torturers-questioners of the Holy Inquisition altered the imagery and put ugly, evil women on brooms. They were in reality beautiful young witches like Joan of Arc. However, they also revered the spirituality and wisdom that age brings, and these women were lovingly and respectfully called crones.

While each tribe or nation assigned different colors and elements to each of the 4 directions, commonly in South America ceremonies began in the south; in North America they began in the east. When you drum or rattle, it is important to call in the energies that you want to be there. Otherwise, it is like going to the corner bar and saying "party at my house."

The following is a version of a journey performed at the time of the full moon in South America called the **"Transformational Fire Ceremony."** Each person brings something to the gathering that will burn that they can offer to the fire to transform or manifest some aspect of themselves. (They may also bring an offering for another.) The aspects or traits are general, such as fear or joy. If everyone states their intent before beginning, a group consciousness is also created; that is, that the intentions of any individual are available for transformation or manifestation by group members. The object that is brought to the fire may represent in some way the goal to be manifested, or the habit or disease that is in need of transformation. The intent could also be written on a piece of paper, or the participant may simply take one of the logs lying next to the fire and throw that in when it is their turn.

Draw the participants into a circle or cast a circle. Then build a safe, friendly fire outside or in your fireplace. Build a friendly fire by adding a few drops of scented oil, or a combination of sage and cedar, or other herbs. Chant, "Wichi - Ti - Ti - Enui - Aurinicka - Aurinicka - Ohhh - Whi." If you prefer, chant another invocation or singing old Bible hymns also works. Sacred Sounds subtitled Transformation through Music & Word by Ted Andrews, and Circle of Song subtitled Songs, Chants and Dances for Ritual and Celebration compiled by Kate Marks are excellent sources. Then meditate on the fire by staring into it. Concentrate on what you want to release or manifest. The individual leading the meditation guides the others:

"In the south see the snake. *(Pause)* What are you releasing? *(Pause)* See it being released as a snake sheds its skin." Meditate!
"In the west see the jaguar. *(Pause)* Look into the mouth and the eyes of the jaguar. *(Pause)* See jaguar's sharp claws. *(Pause)* Die to the old aspect of yourself. See it dying." Meditate!
"In the north see horse or buffalo. *(Pause)* Climb on the back of the animal. *(Pause)* He takes you to the crystal cave where a master sits. *(Pause)* Be with the master. He can answer your questions." Meditate!
"In the east see the Eagle or Condor. *(Pause)* What vision is the bird showing you?" Meditate!

Concentrating on the quality to be manifested or transformed, each person in turn brings up the object they have brought to be burned, cleanses themselves before the fire, and places the object in the fire while the others chant, drum or rattle if they wish. The next day bury the completely cooled ashes in the earth.

The following is a variation of a North American ceremony, **"Morning Star"** (Our Sun) performed as the sun is rising or in the morning. Set up your altar as described above. In addition place the following candles on your altar: Yellow in the east, green in the south, red in the west, white in the north and a pink candle in the center. Call in spiritual energy, "Oh Great Spirit, Mother Earth, Father Sky, the power of the 4 directions, the power of the 4 elements, all my totem animals, all my ancestors, all my spirit guides and helpers, be here with me now!"

Begin in the east and as you light the yellow candle say, "With the lighting of this yellow candle in the east, I call forth the energies of the great Archangel Uriel, the energies of fire, the energies of clarity and purification. Here I honor the life force that keeps this planet green." Burn some sage and cedar and address Great Spirit in this fashion, "You were there when I needed you. You stood above all the rest. With your strength you guided me. To you I offer my love, my being and all that I am."

Face the south, and as you light the green candle say, "With the lighting of this green candle in the south, I call forth the energies of the great Archangel Raphael, the energies of water, the

137

energies of healing and the awakening of my psychic abilities. Here I honor the plant kingdom and blessed herbs." Burn some sage and cedar and address Great Spirit in this fashion, "You were there when I needed you. You stood above all the rest. With your strength you guided me. To you I offer my love, my being and all that I am."

Face the west, and as you light the red candle say, "With the lighting of the red candle in the west, I call forth the energies of the great Archangel Michael, the energies of earth, the energies of grounding, prosperity and prayer. This is the place of the sun trail and the carving out of paths. Here I honor my ancestors, those who have come before me." Burn some sage and cedar and address Great Spirit in this fashion, "You were there when I needed you. You stood above all the rest. With your strength you guided me. To you I offer my love, my being and all that I am."

Face the north, and as you light the white candle say, "With the lighting of this white candle in the north, I call upon the Holy Angelic Host, the energies of air, the energies of wisdom, communication and gratitude. It is here that I come full circle and I offer prayers of thanks to All There Is. It is here that I honor the Great Mystery." Burn some sage and cedar and address Great Spirit in this fashion, "You were there when I needed you. You stood above all the rest. With your strength you guided me. To you I offer my love, my being and all that I am."

Meditate. Feel yellow color coming into your crown from Father Sky, flowing down and through you, out your root chakra and feet, and into Mother Earth. Feel cobalt blue color coming into your root chakra from Mother Earth, flowing up and through you, out the top of your head and into Father Sky. Feel the uniting of Mother-Father God in your heart. When you are through, open your eyes and light the pink candle in the center of the altar. "With the lighting of this pink candle I call forth the energies of the great Archangel Gabriel, the energies of love and compassion. I ask that my heart might become the center of the medicine wheel, that I might be connected to the circle of life, that my life might be a reflection of Your Love and Your Strength so that beauty and harmony might flow through me." If you wish, meditate again and feel the love connection between your third eye and heart chakras, then ground the energy in your navel.

We are supposed to be using the magic found within and around earth to make our lives easier, more enjoyable and so that we might be in flow with the earth, and the cosmos, and the circle of life. In tuning into nature, or learning to use our intuition in nature, we understand ourselves as well as our relationship to the Universe. Miracles should be happening everyday and throughout the day. With changes occurring as we move into the Golden Age, magic, ceremonies and journey work will become increasingly common and necessary.

Color and Healing

The colors are not to be confused with the Seven Rays mentioned in Alice Bailey's material. The Seven Rays originate from the Eternal Sacred Fire and come in on a vibration of color to bring us back into balance. When we are out of balance we are in duality and play the game called pairs of opposites. That is, it is not uncommon for the abused child to become the abuser in adulthood, or the egotist to simultaneously suffer from low self-esteem. The Seven Rays work to resolve and raise the hierarchtical constructs in the aura. That in turn brings the mental and emotional bodies into equalibrium, and lastly the physical comes into alignment. The energy centers in the open heart center, where we are supposed to listen and think from. It is my belief that just as the halo painted above the heads of the saints, Jesus and Mary represents the open crown chakra, the fire often depicted in their hearts represents the Sacred Eternal Flame. Artists are often visionaries; however, in an age of religious fanaticism they disguised spiritual concepts so that they would not be burned as heretics. While they could not speak out, their paintings hung as a reminder to the subconscious and reached out to the soul.

The battle between the sexes is an outward reflection of the war that wages within us. When we balance Shakti (Mother-God, qualities of nurturing, creativity and healing) and Shiva (Father-God, qualities of teacher, consoler and warrior that protects us) in us, we align to the Love of the Christ Light. Clarity allows the kundalini to rise safely, and that in turn brings enlightenment which allows us to see all of the tools God has made available to us, such as the colors. The colors are used in healing and come to us through the Creator's manifestations:

Cobalt blue comes from Mother Earth. In healing it is used for cleansing and nurturing. Cobalt blue comes from the earth and into the open chakras at the soles of the feet. Cobalt blue also comes into the root chakra (if it is clean) and goes up the spine and out the crown. Helps connect our front to our back. Its guardian is Hava, the mother of all living. To use this or any of the colors in healing, we tune into our instincts and we will find what works. Using the colors in this manner also helps to build and strengthen our own intuition.

Emerald green is a color of healing and growth. It connects us to nature and the cosmos and specifically corresponds to the planet Neptune. It is the ray of invisibility because of Neptune's own nearly invisible ring. This ring often eludes the strongest of earth's telescopes. The guardians are Barachiel and El Shaddai. Emerald green comes in through the open heart chakra.

Violet color of transformation helps to remove layer by layer psychic debris. Saint Germane is the guardian. Helps us to work through the last layer of self-denial and to reach core issues. The last layer for many people is self-hatred, which can be manifested in the human body as depression, shame, pain and commonly sinus problems. Behind the sinus problem is a veil of unshed tears. What we are grieving is the love that we have denied to ourselves, which has manifested as disease, pain, fear, and unfulfilled lives. This healing color comes in through the crown and solar plexus.

Orange was the first healing color on planet earth. Orange is a color of manifestation, and it is like fire in that fire represents both birth and death. Flames burn away the old, but from the ashes, like the phoenix, rises new life. Its guardian is Buddha. Orange comes in through the 2nd or creative chakra and the throat.

Blue-green is the color of the sea, and within this ray can be found lost knowledge. Representative of blood, origin, turning back time and youth. Regenerative color because we come from the sea. Kelp is a good herb to take 3 times a day for a whole week before the initiation into the colors, because it, too, is regenerative. Initiations require that the initiated be respectful of not only the energy, but of the source of that energy, the sea. This color comes into the healer through the soles of the feet and the mouth. Ceasa is the guardian.

Pink is a color of Compassion and connects us to the ascended masters. Pink comes into the body through the open heart. It directly corresponds to Venus and indirectly to Jupiter. Its element is both air and earth, and it is supple and soft by nature. It represents love, growth, healing, jewelry and the finer things of life. With the subjugation of women, this ray left Mother Earth and is now returning in its pure form. Gabriel is the guardian.

Ruby Red, the color of Christ Consciousness is used in centering and in healing the past; thus, it is transformative in nature. It is the ray of forgiveness and new beginnings. Ruby red has the elements of both unconditional love and passion. This color comes into the body through the root and crown chakras. Michael is the guardian.

Yellow is associated with the sun and is a masculine, spontaneous, carefree energy. It represents growth, giving and friendship. In healing it aids us with our spiritual growth through enlightenment. Yellow comes in through the solar plexus and 3rd eye. Because the 3rd eye is indigo, the color the the evening sky, yellow also connects us with nocturnal animals. It may be the reason behind why the Mayans had a totem animal for both the sun during the day and the hidden sun at night. Uriel is the guardian.

Crystalline white color connects and unifies. Center of information and guidance. Representation of the One. White comes from the All and comes into the healer through all of the chakras. Receiver as well as a sender because it is a focus of all colors. With all of the colors, but especially this one, it is important to send back energy and thanks after we receive. In healing the healer focuses and sends crystalline white color to the healee, while the healee meditates within and focuses on a point within the brain, the pituitary gland.

Black represents all lost knowledge, and the hidden mystery which is within us and draws us to the knowledge of the One. We cannot draw upon something which draws us, we can only bring it forth; thus, there is no point correlation in the body for black except the brain, specifically in the pituitary gland. Black is unlimited energy, and it is an absorber of misqualified energy. The pituitary is not only the master gland for the physical body, but it is through the pituitary that auditory and visual messages from other dimensions are processed. The vertical energy line that runs through us is next to our pituitary gland, and it is through this gland that we can access our own seat of consciousness. Babaji is the master of this ray.

The initiation and integration into the colors and the Seven Rays is done in a 2-day shamanic ritual. Workshop participants are taught how to journey, shamanic soul retrieval, and how use shamanic work in hands-on-healing. Ama Deus (I love God) is also included. It is a healing, magic and divination system which has been used for thousands and thousands of years by the shamans of the Guaranis tribe in the central jungle of Brazil.

Initiation

Tremendous changes on earth are having ramifications throughout the universe and beyond. Leaving the Piscean Age behind and entering the Aquarian, we are just now completing the 25,960 year procession of the 12 astrological houses. Five-hundred and twenty years of darkness and ignorance began when Cortez assassinated the high priest and ended March 21, 1969. With the ending of the these cycles we are presently in the process of moving into a great golden age and the return of angels, which is why there is currently so much interest in them.

Matriarchies coerce men; patriarchies, as the one we have been living in, subjugate women. When women are diminished the 1/3 feminine aspect of nurturing, creativity and intuition within men is buried and not fully expressed. Renunciation of females produces tension between men and women resulting in polarized relationships and the disruption of the family. What people view today as the tearing apart of 'family values' is nothing new, it is simply taking on another form. The Church used to advise husbands to beat their wives at least once a week to keep them in line. Dysfunctional behavior does not produce love and healthy relationships. Today, women's liberation results in domestic tension whenever the wife has two jobs, one outside of the home and the other inside of the the home taking care of the children and the household, while the father still has one. I have worked on several women whose mental and emotional fatigue, and physical ailments are directly the result of sheer exhaustion. For some working wives, their husbands won't even pick up their dirty dishes when they are through eating and carry them to the sink.

Piscean method of learning was through pain and separation. It didn't have to be this way but, for whatever reason, it was. Aquarian lessons will be learned through groups. Aquarian relationships will form that support and contribute to group consciousness. We will look at what is good for the whole rather than, "How can I or a few people prosper at the expense of earth and everyone else?" Possibilities for individual soul growth will be in retaining the expression of individuality, which is the tension point of the Aquarian Age. Paradoxically, we have been, are, and always will be a part of the Oneness, and at the same time unique. Both of these aspects are vital to a healthy soul. Healthy souls reflect back and live in healthy worlds.

Healing the wounds between men and women, and opening up to both our feminine and masculine attributes has been referred to by some as becoming androgynous. That in itself sounds a bit like Mr. Milktoast. Reality is that we will be opening to the 1/3-2/3 balance of feminine/ masculine or masculine/feminine energies that are within us all.

Homosexuality has been a perfectly valid way in the Eye of God to learn and grow. It is not a sin! To stand on a podium or pulpit and blame homosexuals for society's ills is a Hitler-type technique which keeps us from looking at and correcting the source of the problem, which is ultimately ourselves. Furthermore, people who 'bash' homosexuals are only seeing in them something similar that they do not want to look at in themselves. We can only see who we are!

One man, who is gay in this lifetime, was shown by his angels that in his past life he was a high officer in the pentagon. In one instance while he was reviewing the troops, the thought crossed his mind that perhaps Hitler was right. His hatred of homosexuals in that lifetime drew him to incarnating as one in this lifetime. We are all drawn to the things we love as well as to the things we despise and judge. Another man became a homosexual later in life so that his harsh and abrasive masculinity could be softened by working exclusively with the feminine aspect.

Homosexuality is typically self hatred pushed to the extreme, in that either the male or female aspect of self is closed to expression. When we deny our own male or female nature, we deny and are in contempt of either the Mother-God or Father-God within us. Then in only working with 1/3 of the personality, a distorted perception of the feminine or masculine occurs. Distortions and inversions occur whenever we are out of balance, for whatever the reason.

As the planets shift, as the cycles change, the spirit of the times will bring many homosexuals back into balance. Vibrating only a portion of our personality into the golden age will not work. We will not be able, for example, to bring our feminine side into the golden age and leave the masculine behind in a 3-dimensional world. As more and more Light comes to Mother Earth on a daily basis, our hidden issues and agendas become heavier and heavier burdens. None of us are going to have an easy time opening blockages and releasing constraints that bind us and hold us back. We all have our issues in one form or another and the dams we have built are breaking!

At the heart of all our issues are inversions, denials, misconceptions, distortions and omissions, which we mask with humor, sophistication and overwork. Behind the mask, problems fester, causing disease, pain, fear, depression and anxiety. When we have the courage to unmask and let the love and Light shine in, we can embrace both the Mother and Father God as well as our own true essence, which we find within. It is in this state of consciousness where we can find the humility to relinquish our control and allow God's Love, Joy, Creativity, etc. to flow through us.

First we have to get past our denials, and that is often not easy to do. For example, a man once asked me if I would help him do a past life regression. When I walked over to the pool later to

142

tell him that I was ready, as he walked up the grotto pool stairs, I suddenly saw him as a masculine Roman soldier in full regalia. When I regressed him shortly thereafter, it wasn't a surprise to me when we ended up in Rome. This particular man was so in denial of his masculine nature that he could not see or feel for himself who he was in that lifetime. He kept talking about his male lover, and I kept seeing his own frustrated maleness trying to get through, "Female lover, not male!" All past lives are experienced through our present brain, and there wasn't anything that I could do to guide his experience past his denial (<u>I am not there to dismiss his experience, only to give suggestions so that he can get to the Truth.</u>) When he came out of trance, he told me that he had also had a Mayan astrology reading that day. In Mayan astrology we do not have one sign, but five. One in the center, one to our left (feminine side), one to our right (masculine side), one in front (where we are going) and one in back (where we have been). He told me that Ken Johnson had told him that he had a <u>strong</u> male presence in back of him. In order to go forward he needed to address his masculine past. What he didn't get was that the male aspect of his personality wanted to be incorporated into his beingness.

The following is not a lip service, and is not going to sit well for most of us. It is based upon the work of Dr. Norberto R. Keppe, president of the International Society of Analytical Trilogy, and the author of <u>Liberation</u>. The numbers are part of sacred geometry, and a system of tap touch points on the human body called the Gems of Excellence channeled and designed by Dorothy Espiau. Charlotte Liss and Sean Grealy designed this formula for the purpose of recognizing and integrating our shadow side so that we can accept and love ourselves for being human. If we cannot accept our negative manifestations, then we cannot accept our Light. Not accepting makes us contract our love and our life; it's what makes our bodies sick. We cannot push our kill away and hope that it disappears. If we push away our shadow, we push away our Light. We cannot repress one side without repressing the other. Because we are in duality and blind to our Oneness, when we cannot work out Luciferian pacts of destruction (resentments, fears, murder and mayhem, etc.) in the world, then we turn it to self destruction, which manifests as pain, disease and unfulfilled and unhappy lives. <u>To integrate power and love to form beauty and harmony:</u>

Cone the fingers of your right hand and circle clockwise *(which will seem counterclockwise to you)* over your chest *(big circles)* and say, "8-7-3-1-2-9-5-7 to integrate the Hitler in me. 8-7-3-1-2-9-5-7 to dissipate the murder, denial, omissions, inversions, distortions and misconceptions in me. 8-7-3-1-2-9-5-7 to integrate this Truth at the deepest neurological and cellular level so that it will be 100% effective and in divine order for this body's highest good. 8-7-3-1-2-9-5-7 for all anchors, locks and seals (poke your left shoulder with your coned fingers). 8-7-3-1-2-9-5-7 for print and save (slash your left shoulder down to your armpit with your coned fingers)."

<u>For those individuals who are working out their Luciferian pacts in the world, they should substitute the word "love" for "Hitler."</u> Power without love is what we call evil run rampant; love without power is what we call Mr. Milktoast. I wonder if this integration of love and power to form beauty and harmony is what the bible refers to as, "and the lion shall lie down with the lamb . . . and peace shall reign o'er all the earth"?

Upcoming changes confuse and allure us. In order to have a glimmering of an understanding of what is about to happen, let's look at a society, who 3,000 years ago perfectly understood where we are coming from and where we are going. Those who grasped the workings and the mind of the cosmos, the Mayans.

Mayan civilization in all aspects was advanced far beyond the comparable European culture of the day. When present historians point to the Mayan human sacrifices, they fail in the same breath to discuss the 11,000,000 people who were murdered by the Roman Catholic Church as supposed witches and heretics. When the Spanish landed, the great Mayan cultural centers, schools and cities had been left abandoned two to three-hundred years earlier. Spaniards literally rewrote Mayan history; they had to in order to justify their actions. For example, Spanish soldiers never witnessed a ball game. When they saw the reliefs on the ball court walls of the team's captain being decapitated, they assumed that it had to be the captain of the loosing team, and that the act was a punishment. In fact it was just the opposite. Captains of winning teams were allowed to die at their highest moment of achievement and glory for their benefit and the benefit of all society. In addition, early Spaniards burned thousands of Mayan texts and books to obliterate the truth and to vindicate their horrific acts performed in what they proclaimed was the name of Jesus.

The high Mayans abandoned their cities because they knew that the dark age was coming. At the same time the Anasazi of southwestern United States and Angor Wat of Cambodia also disappeared. Millions of highly evolved people simultaneously vanished off the surface of the planet. Not wanting their energy and advancements to be misused by future people fixated on power and wealth, they took their advanced metaphysical knowledge off the planet. Mayans, Anasazi, and Angor Wat vibrated into another dimension or parallel universe.

Mayan spiritualism cannot be understood by western mental constructs. To be Mayan is not a color of skin, it is a state of consciousness. To the Mayans knowledge belongs only to the memory of God or Hunab'ku. We are held in the memory of Kunaku. We are God because we have memory. To go within, to meditate, is to go into God Consciousness. The more understanding we have, the closer we are to God. We become like Buddha or Christ.

In the memory of God, when something is finished, it is finished! God speaks and it is! The age of darkness is over with! It began when Cortez assassinated the high priest and ended March 21, 1969. We are only experiencing the residue from the Dark Age. To continue with a technology 'hell bent' on profit at any cost and by any means would bring final destruction to Earth if allowed to continue. While the forces of 'evil' had its way for 520 years, the Law of Cycles and the Spirit of the Times now says, "No!" What used to work here, doesn't work here anymore! That's what's different about the times we are now living in. In this period it is speaking out the Truth and taking action on behalf of the Truth that saves us.

Movement is currently towards balance, whereby we honor Mother Earth and utilize the best of technology, which up to this point has not been allowed to develop for the benefit of humanity. Neither the human sacrifice of the matriarchy, nor the death and destruction through war of the patriarchy will exist in the golden age, a state of equilibrium. Mother-Father God, as will we all, be in balance and in unity. We will be in an expanded state of consciousness and awareness from which we will be able to explore the universe, our potential, and co-create with Mother-Father God. Ancient Mayan prophesy gave March 21, 1995 as the beginning of the new age.

Nature was the Mayan's teacher. Trees were considered teachers and protectors. Mayans also understood that we are a reflection of the cosmos. Our human body's relationship to the cosmos is described in detail in The Occult Anatomy of Man by Hall. It is yet one more way we in this holographic universe are in dynamic relationship to All There Is. In Truth what happens to one of us affects us all.

Mayan day keepers, like Humbatz Men, who wrote Secrets of Mayan Science/Religion, are in the process of revealing long kept hidden secrets to help humanity's evolvement into the golden age. According to this Mayan shaman, in the Mayan religion the sun and its life force was the physical manifestation of divine Light. Eagle represented the sun during the day; jaguar the hidden sun at night. Carvings in the Mayan temples of the eagle and jaguar holding human hearts do not represent two warrior factions, like the army and the air force. Rather they speak of the love and devotion from the heart that is mandatory as a precursor to high spiritual work. The heart is the fulcrum between what we refer to as the lower emotions and the upper emotions, with the third eye being the center for Buddha or Christ consciousness. Love from the heart stimulates the brain and opens the third eye. The heart is the gateway to higher psychic

145

development. Without heart love energy, evolvement of the higher faculties is unattainable. In retrospect it is one of the fail-safes that Mother-Father God has instituted to keep conferred power from those who would abuse it.

To be Quetzalcoatal or Kulkulcan, the feathered serpent, is to be initiated with spiritual knowledge and empowerment, and to be able to manifest through these faculties. In other words, make the invisible visible. The true initiate is balanced between the heavens and the earth, and has a perfect understanding of energy. To the Mayans the beautiful Quetzal birds perfectly represented these spiritual concepts. The male's brilliant ruby red breast and long emerald green tail feathers were a sight to behold. In flight, with his undulating tail, he looked like a flying snake. Snake was closest to earth, bird nearest to the sun. Thus, Quetzals physically represented the knowledge, integration and mastery of the Laws of heaven and earth. Mayans also knew that energy, as well as the cosmos, moves in a wave-like motion like the undulating, crawling snake and the quetzal in flight. Temple reliefs of the image of the initiate's head inside the mouth of the snake represents transformation, like the snake shedding its skin, like the initiate's own transformation.

The act of going through physically, mentally and emotionally demanding initiations which the Mayans, Egyptians and Native Americans endured in itself prepares the initiate. In the case of an energy transfer, like Shakti Pac or Reiki, the initiation plants a seed. It is up to the individual to develop that energy through meditation and practice. Further, it is up to the individual to own the initiation. I know of 2 cases where the initiate disavowed later that the energy transfer had taken place. In both instances Yahweh said, "Yes!" If the ego is inflated with unprecedented self-worth or if the initiated dishonors their teacher or the energy, then there is no room for initiation.

Shakti Pac is an energy transfer to the spine of the initiate. As the nerves carry psychic energy, the spinal cord is an appropriate initiation point. This initiation is like sitting at the Roulette table in Las Vegas, but everyone is a winner in Shakti Pac. However, not everyone receives the same amount of energy in the transfer. Spirit determines what each initiate gets, not the initiator.

Reiki initiations utilize a specific series of physical acts and symbols by the initiator. In this way everyone receives the same initiation, everyone receives the same energy. With each of the 3 Reiki initiations *(Sai Baba told me that there are only 3 Reiki initiations)* the crown chakra is expanded to receive more Reiki healing energy. The initiator needs to know the process, and be able to hold and transfer the full Universal energy of the initiation. <u>If the initiator does not know the correct procedure, or does not or is unable to hold the energy then the full energy transfer does not occur</u>.

There are many people who can heal, but neither know how to, or are capable of transferring the energy. I know of one individual who has nothing good to say about Reiki, yet his own students are unable to do the same kinds of healings that this individual can. Before I study with any teacher I look to see what his or her students are doing.

Universal energy is just that. It is neither the master-teacher's energy, nor does it come from Japan or Tibet. Universal healing energy is carried within rays emanating from Source. Each initiation carries its own particular vibration. Brian Johnson told me that he felt like hot liquid gold was being poured into his crown during the **Sakara** initiations. For many initiates, the first initiation into fire is memorable. I was told that the first Sakara initiation is equivalent in energy to the Seichem Mastership initiation.   It is our nerves which carry the psychic and healing energy. The masters and angelic beings, who are ultimately the ones doing the initiations through the initiator, also have to make adjustments in the initiated healer so that the nerves do not become brittle. I have both experienced this phenomenon myself and watched these highly evolved beings as they work on those whom I am initiating.

People who have been initiated into **Cahokia** experience a cold beyond anything they have ever felt before. It is this same freezing aspect which works in healing to isolate, numb and heal diseased tissue. When the miracles occur I am dissociated from my body, I am the silent observer watching another aspect of myself diligently working with the Holy Spirits. The seer in me is the observer of the process. Yet, even with the Cahokia, if the issues behind the disease, pain and behavior are not addressed, the healing is a temporary quick fix.

Almost 200 years ago in colonial Pennsylvania, Joseph Smith found golden tables inscribed in ancient Hebrew writing. According to these tablets Jesus performed his greatest miracle by raising his body from the dead. Afterwards he did not ascend, rather he walked the earth. Messiah means the chosen one; chosen to lead us out of unconsciousness and back to Wholeness. It does not mean the only son of God, which Jesus never claimed to be. It was the Roman Catholic Church who voted by one ballot to make Jesus divine (Peter De Rosa <u>The Vicars of Christ, The Dark Side of the Papacy</u>). Leaving some of his disciples behind in Jerusalem, Jesus and some of his other followers sailed for the Americas and landed in what is now known as Cancoon, Mexico. All of the native American tribes have a legend about a white man with reddish brown hair who could walk on water, raise the dead, and perform other miracles. It is no coincidence that 2,000 years ago White Buffalo Calf Woman appeared to the nations to teach them the ways of the spirit. Could she have been one of Jesus' disciples? (The original teachings of Jesus speak of how he did have women whom he taught as disciples.) Like other religions before them, the Mormans were gifted with the power and the knowledge of the **Order of Melchizedek**. One of the Gifts of the Spirit is healing others (Corinthians 12 verses 8-11). The Mormons altered the teachings to fit their own patriarchal ideas, and the Golden Tablets disappeared shortly thereafter. When the clergy in general no longer do healings, we have to ask ourselves, why?

Throughout the bible there is mention of an ancient priesthood, the Order of Melchizedek, which dates back to before the time of Abraham. The initiation itself connects one to the Divine plan for earth and the Ancient Ones, initiates a natural flow into life, and is a foundation for healing. Everyone receives something in a Reiki initiation; with the Order of Melchizedek, either you get it or you don't. When I am doing these initiations, the sensation is like being in a spaceship. I am surrounded by a ring of lights. If someone in the group is not getting the initiation, there will be a blank space in the circle. I will not embarrass them by stating that they haven't gotten it, they usually know for themselves. This is not a judgement, rather it simply means that they have work to do on themselves before they are able to receive this energy.

Most people who receive the initiation into the Order of Melchizedek begin at level 22. Those who have worked with this energy in prior lifetimes are initiated into level 33. The energy progresses in double-digit numbers (Master numbers) through meditation and right action. When Jesus started his ministry he was at level 77. Again, as with other healing energy, no one can initiate someone into something that they do not have. The Order of Melchizedek is evidenced by the healing the initiate does. "Ye shall know them by their works!" This initiation is accomplished by using the human energy field as a magnet to draw in and ground electromagnetic energy which aids in drawing in both cobalt blue from Mother Earth, and yellow from the sun.

The Order of Melchizedek helps to ground and increases the flow of the **elemental healing rays**. With each initiation into an elemental healing ray, a crucial 21-day cleansing cycle is initiated which begins at the root chakra and lasts for a full 24 hours. The second day the cycle moves to the second chakra and works there for 24 hours. At the seventh day the energy will be at the crown; at the eighth day it will be back at the root chakra. Thus, there are three clearings of the seven major chakras. The initiate is wide open and it is an excellent opportunity to release 'stuff'. Jane Rijgersberg in Holland has found that for those who wish to hold on, they will only attract more 'stuff'. For example, one man had lost all of the fillings in his teeth. At the fifth day the energy reached his throat and mouth and went no further because he could not look at the issues behind his dental problems. The initiation did not take!

Babaji told me that an initiation should be given in its entirety. For example, when I was initiated into the first degree of Reiki my teacher did the 4 initiation points, crown, third eye, throat and heart separately. At the end of the first day we were warned to be careful in our activities, especially in driving because we were out of balance. Babaji also told me that all of the initiations were best begun at the crown since that is where the Universal energy was coming into the initiate. Initiations should be done one on one. One group initiation is possible; however, if even one person holds themselves back, then everyone in the group is held back.

I leave the time period between initiations up to each individual. Some people will only do Reiki I. At the other end of the spectrum, for those people who manage to do Reiki I, II and III within a week's time. These are souls who have worked with this energy in other lifetimes and I am only helping them to remember. There are people who come long distances to receive Sakara and the other rays of touch healing, and who also know that they want to do all three initiations. For their convenience, I do the initiations one after the other. Masters and angels stack the initiations one on top of another above their crown. After the initiation I ask them to have their angels and guides show them the initiations above their crown so that they will have their own knowing. All they have to do after the 21-day cleansing, when they are ready, is to meditate and bring the next energy combination that is above their crown into their consciousness and body.

The masters have asked me not to show anyone how to do these initiations until after the school has been established. Many people have walked away when they found out that if they went through the initiations, that they would not be able to be independent teachers. I believe that the Master's intention has been to gather a group of people whose primary focus is healing. As we evolve upwards into higher and higher levels, we have all been tested.

Of all of the many angel initiations that are available, there is a series of initiations that actually goes back to **Enochian Magic**, which the Church derived from Jesus' original teachings. There actually have been popes who were Enochian Magicians. The 3 physical initiations cleanse the physical body, opens the psychic channels and prepares the healer as a vessel for healing energy. The second and third initiations open and widen the etheric spine so that any rays of healing that are coming into the crown can be moved quickly through the healer and into the healee. It is the difference between sending energy through a household appliance wire and an industrial coil. The open, powerful root chakra grounds the healing. It is interesting to note that the symbols used in each of the 3 initiations can be likened to an equal-armed cross. The initiation connects the initiate to the astral plane and the angelic realm.

When Atlantis broke up, the esoteric mysteries were scattered as well. Buddha, Jesus, Dr. Usui and other masters were able to piece back within themselves the multidimensional aspects of healing. It is the combination of healing rays, serving as a vessel and higher communication that allowed Jesus to heal through holy archangels and the Holy Angelic Host. Jesus experienced not only the Egyptian initiations but others as well. The original gospels speak of this.

There are several variations of **3rd eye initiations** which have been done in various mystery schools including Wiccan magic. The initiations typically involve drawing symbols over the third eye to help the chakra to cleanse and open. If the initiator is capable of transferring Universal Energy from Source, that too occurs. In the highest initiation, the crown is opened, and there is a connection that is made for the the initiated between the 3rd eye and the heart. It is this combination which enables all of the psychic centers to open. It is beneficial to receive this initiation at varying intervals as the third eye opens slowly.

Initiations received in high states of meditation by angels and masters must be made physical. In order to take physical form, there must be a physical action. Initiation through an initiator is not the only way. Mikao Usui was struck in his third eye by lightening. Zev Kohlman was able to channel healing energy after he was struck by lightening in Israel on Mt. Sinai. Native shaman had their ordeals. People who have had near death experiences or other traumatic experiences sometimes are able to heal, or their psychic centers are opened when they return to their bodies or health. Correspondingly, their whole lives often change.

I had to make the effort to manifest the knowledge and healing empowerment given to me over an eight-year period by the masters and angels. I have studied with many teachers, and have gone through minor and major initiations. I have visited places of empowerment, and places where I have lived in other lifetimes. As I told my friend-student-teacher, Sage at Ishpiming, "The Universe is not a cheap date!" She agrees!

As I am involved in a process (and I believe that this is true for all teachers in my position), those people whom I have initiated are connected to me in such a way, that as I go up in energy, they do so likewise. Those few who disconnect themselves, do so when they dishonor the energy through misuse or nonpayment. They invalidate their own certificates.

In my travels and studies, not always, but often I and my fellow students and initiates are told by the instructor that the healing energy that they are working with cannot be mixed with any other energies. All healing comes from the Creator, and if I have been initiated into it, it will flow through me on its own accord. Healing energy works with all techniques; it is what makes the techniques effective. When we put our own limited perceptions on Universal Energy, we bind it and constrict the flow. I can call upon a particular energy or raise my arms and pull it in, which will increase its intensity; however, if the energy is not what is needed, it will not come. Holy Spirit is intelligent! Actually, when healing modalities and energies are combined, they become multidimensional and thus more beneficial.

Initiations are not the only way to work with psychic and healing energy. Individuals who journey through life seeking truth, love, wisdom and empowerment certainly accumulate universal elemental life force energy. Other people are born with this energy.

What is happening right now, as the veil between the 3rd and 4th dimension becomes thinner and thinner, is that more and more people are coming in contact with their spiritual gifts, or know that there is something else out there besides survival in a 3-D world. When we begin to question dogmas, read objectively, and seek out teachers, we find our own truth. That is, that we are one with the circle of life, we are a part of the Wholeness of All There Is.

It is difficult for me to end this book, I have been working on it for so long. Perhaps on a very practical note, so that I do not receive bags of mail from every western rider in the country, I should say that western saddles are a legitimate way of riding a horse, it's just not my way. Yes, when I was riding down a mountain outside of Tucson it was very good to have a saddle horn between me and ground that was perhaps a thousand feet below us.

I will leave you with a horse poem of sorts which Abez gave to me not long ago.

Two twin stars standing in the night sky,
Always together, never apart.
Silvery flight, thundering hoof beats,
Passageway home, you are in my heart.
Light, Light and rebirth, not in hay but
Frolicking in Timothy, clover.
Wobbly, white colt with rainbow light wings,
To the new one, Hava, look over.

151

Mail Order for video and audio tapes:
Kathleen Milner
9600 North 96th Street, Box 219
Scottsdale, Arizona   85258

Videos

<u>$35 each</u> (includes handling and U.S. postage)

Your favorite retail store may order most of these tapes for you at the same price.

See description of 3 companion videos on back cover of this book.

Reiki Mastership is available and useful to those individuals who have taken the class.

Audio Tapes

<u>$11 each</u> (includes handling and U.S. postage)

Candle Meditation   Meditator guided into the "gap" between thought and breath through spiritual techniques taught in ancient mystery schools. Some meditators can hear and experience the qualities of Angeliclight. <u>Crystal Cave</u> on side 2 is an inward journey to places of healing and self empowerment.

Journey to Sacred Mountain   Incorporates the 4 directions, 4 elements, and Mother-Father God into our own heart centers which is where sacred mountain lies. <u>Ancient Symbology</u> on side 2 works with Universal archetypal energies found within Egyptian hieroglyphs.

When the Angels Came   Healing journey with angels to the vortexes and power places on Mother Earth. <u>Passageways</u>, music only by Richard Bennett on side 2.

Atlantian Heart Chakra Meditation   Group meditation using candles and combined consciousness to explore other realities and to bring back healing for the members of the group and for Mother Earth. <u>Atlantis</u>, music only by Paul Lincoln on side 2.

Past Life Regression   Begins with a healing meditation for the physical body. <u>Shaman's Journey</u> on side 2 is a meditation with colors, symbols and the shaman's drum.

Entire series consisting of the book, <u>Reiki & Other Rays of Touch Healing</u>, 3 companion videos, and 5 audio tapes retails for $165. **ISBN 1-886903-99-9**